Building up
the Body

Text copyright © Richard Steel 2013
The author asserts the moral right
to be identified as the author of this work

Published by
The Bible Reading Fellowship
15 The Chambers, Vineyard
Abingdon, OX14 3FE
United Kingdom
Tel: +44 (0)1865 319700
Email: enquiries@brf.org.uk
Website: www.brf.org.uk
BRF is a Registered Charity

ISBN 978 0 85746 175 9

First published 2013

10 9 8 7 6 5 4 3 2 1 0

Acknowledgments

Unless otherwise stated, scripture quotations taken from The Holy Bible, New International Version (Anglicised edition) copyright © 1973, 1978, 1984, 2011 by Biblica (formerly International Bible Society). Used by permission of Hodder & Stoughton Publishers, an Hachette UK company. All rights reserved. 'NIV' is a registered trade mark of Biblica (formerly International Bible Society). UK trademark number 1448790.

Scripture quotations from *THE MESSAGE*. Copyright © by Eugene H. Peterson 1993, 1994, 1995. Used by permission of NavPress Publishing Group.

Scripture quotations marked NLT are taken from the Holy Bible, New Living Translation, copyright © 1996, 2004. Used by permission of Tyndale House Publishers, Inc., Wheaton, Illinois 60189. All rights reserved.

Extracts from the Authorised Version of the Bible (The King James Bible), the rights in which are vested in the Crown, are reproduced by permission of the Crown's patentee, Cambridge University Press.

A catalogue record for this book is available from the British Library

The paper used in the production of this publication was supplied by mills that source their raw materials from sustainable managed forests. Soy-based inks were used in its printing and the laminate film is biodegradable.

Printed in Singapore by Craft Print International Ltd

Building up the Body

Encouraging, equipping and enabling volunteers in the church

Richard Steel

Preface

I owe so much to the many volunteers I have had the pleasure to work with over the years. Without them the churches and organisations for whom I have worked would be so much less successful. That is the first reason I wanted to write this book, as a kind of extended 'thank you' to all the volunteers I have known.

A second reason, equally important, is that I want to encourage the good practice that will make the lives of volunteers better and their contribution more valuable. I have known some good volunteers who have been disheartened by the way they have been treated. My hope is that through sharing what I have learnt others may become better leaders of volunteers, whether they are volunteers themselves or are paid. The latter have a special duty towards those they lead since, as well as giving their time, the volunteers are often providing the money that pays for their leaders. That is true of churches but equally of many Christian organisations and indeed many charities, large and small.

A third reason is that almost all of the books currently available on church-based volunteering are American, and many of them are written from the experience of churches with far larger programmes and budgets than most UK churches have at their disposal.

And the final reason is 'that the Body of Christ may be built up' (Ephesians 4:12) and may be more effective in its mission.

I have approached the task with a great deal of trepidation. I am very aware that in much of what follows I am encouraging an ideal; that those volunteers who work with me have every right to say, 'Physician, heal thyself!' (Luke 4:23, KJV). All I offer in my defence is that I have always sought to learn from my mistakes and that I am doing my best to continue to improve in accordance with best practice as I have researched and reflected in preparation for writing this book. There are times when I get it right and times when I get it wrong, like most leaders of volunteers. I have been encouraged over the years by the amount of positive response I have had, and absolutely delighted when people have said my leadership has led them to experience a new level of satisfaction or opened up new vistas of service. I also know how often I fall short of my aspirations. As a Christian minister I can speak enthusiastically of the value of seeking forgiveness and encourage you to do the same if anything you read here triggers guilt.

At a recent workshop on volunteering we were asked to line up in order of how long we have been involved in leading volunteers and, after a few moments' thought, I realised that this had been far longer than my time in professional ministry. I went back to the time when I was a Junior Leader in the Scouts (and even a Sixer in the Cubs). I have trained volunteers in local churches during my time in radio broadcasting and in my wider roles for the church at diocesan and national levels. As Communication Director for the Church Mission Society (CMS) I worked with many of the volunteers who were at its heart, leading the team responsible for the support and resourcing of their entire volunteer network. I am now the rector of a parish church in which volunteers do the great majority of the work. I chair a local community group that is run entirely by volunteers and a national group of volunteers that produces booklets on leadership. Alongside this I have had academic opportunities to study leadership. In effect, I have been formally volunteering since I was twelve (a lot earlier if you count 'Bob-a-Job') in a variety of one-off and regular roles.

It is from this experience that I offer these insights, along with my grateful thanks to the large number of volunteers, many of them good friends, whose wisdom and support I value so much. You will find some of their stories here. All the examples I use in the book are real, either from my own experience or from those of colleagues. Some names and details have been changed to avoid identification and save any embarrassment.

Contents

Introduction 8

1 Why people volunteer—and what it offers them in return..... 13

2 Understanding today's volunteers 21

3 Building up the Body of Christ.. 35

4 Wider ways of volunteering.. 46

5 Recruiting your volunteers 58

6 Teams, training, trust—and taking risks............................. 75

7 A word to leaders... 85

8 The professional problem... 99

9 Practicalities... 112

10 Saying 'thank you' 123

11 Problems, conflict and ending well................................... 133

12 Beyond the church walls... 150

Afterword: the story continues 154

Appendix 1: Web resources... 155

Appendix 2: Sample policies 163

Notes.. 167

Introduction

Katherine is someone who takes her Christian commitment very seriously. A regular worshipper, she leads our Friday night children's group, is part of the team for Sunday club, and helps lead the annual holiday club. For some years she has been regularly leading family services and been a Baptism preparation visitor with her husband. She is currently on a three-year training course to become a licensed worship leader. Following helping on a Christian basics course, she is now leading a house group. On some Saturday nights she is part of a 'Street Angels' team (a network of people who help those made vulnerable through drink or drugs, who've had accidents, need a coffee, or help to get home while out in the town). She is on a couple of church committees. Oh, yes, and she's a full-time teacher and has been acting Deputy Head!

Katherine might be at one end of the spectrum of volunteering, but volunteers of all sorts are key to the life of the church. The following roles are carried out in my church by volunteers:

- Churchwardens (elders)
- Church Council, including officers such as treasurer and secretary
- Large proportion of the day-to-day pastoral support of the congregation
- All the youth and children's work
- Majority of pre-Baptism preparation
- The general wedding preparation
- Almost all bereavement follow-up
- A good proportion of the leading of worship and preaching
- All the music in worship (apart from a paid organist at funerals and weddings)
- Leading of house groups

- Almost all visiting of elderly, housebound and hospital visiting
- Lunch club for older people
- Fundraising
- Project management for our church development project
- Production of the church magazine
- Website
- Bell-ringing
- Church flowers
- And many more...

Even though in my church we are fortunate currently to have two full-time clergy and a part-time administrator, along with some paid cleaning and caretaking hours, by far the largest proportion of work is still done by volunteers. This is true across most churches, of whatever size and resources. The church simply could not exist and have developed in the way it has without volunteers. This is not just about running activities. It is about the church's mission.

Typical dictionary definitions of volunteering include 'freely offering to do something' or 'working for an organisation without being paid'. The Cabinet Office defines volunteering a little more thoroughly as 'any non-compulsory activity which involves spending time, unpaid, doing something which is of benefit to others (excluding relatives), society or the environment.'[1]

I would go further. Many volunteers are doing what they do for the love of those they serve, whether face to face or more indirectly, and the love of the cause or the activity. Love is a key driver for volunteering, even if not every volunteer might describe it in that way. In my mind there is a strong link between the word 'volunteer' and the word 'amateur'. Both refer to activities done without payment, with the latter (coming as it does from the Latin for 'to love') being about the 'why' rather than the 'what'. As a Christian, it is my love for God and people that drives me to volunteer. The kind of love we are talking of here is that expressed by the Greek *agape* (as used in 1 Corinthians 13), which I define as 'promise love'. It is an act of the will, spiritual and selfless, very appropriate when one thinks about what a volunteer does. Although this passage is most often referred to within wedding services, we should remember its original context. Paul includes this poetic chapter within a discussion on relationships in the church, relationships that were not of the best. It comes in the midst of some stern words about what happens when things go wrong in the life of a congregation. Without love we have no life within the church. Without loving service we have no mission.

Paul is addressing volunteers. The Church was founded by volunteers, those who gave everything freely, who met and cared for one another (Acts 2:44–46; 6:1–5). Paul was himself a volunteer, for at least some of his ministry (Acts 18:3; 1 Corinthians 9:12–17), and encouraged others to give both money (Romans 12:8; 1 Corinthians 16:1–2) and service for others (Acts 20:35). Throughout history there have been people who have given up much for the sake of the gospel and worked tirelessly without receiving payment, mostly completely unknown.

Building people up as volunteers is not just for the benefit of our individual churches nor just for their personal development. It is about playing our small part in building up God's kingdom, enabling the church to reach out into all walks of society, all professions, all networks. It is about giving people skills and experiences that make them better people *for God* and his mission in the world. Even the 'Universal Declaration on Volunteering' of 2001, a secular charter, recognises a spiritual aspect to volunteering. It calls on religious groups 'to affirm volunteering as an appropriate response to the spiritual call to all people to serve'.[2] We talk a lot about 'vocation' (the posh word for 'calling') in the church. Too often that seems limited to those who go abroad in mission or enter full-time church work, teaching or the medical professions. In fact, all church members have a calling from God, in their work and in their volunteering.

My favourite picture of the church is that of the Body (Romans 12:4–5; 1 Corinthians 10:17; 12:12–31; Ephesians 4:4–6). It's a Body in which every person plays their part; a Body in which each has gifts and no one is useless; a Body called to work for the sake of God and his kingdom; and a Body in which so many do so much, and only a very few of us get paid for the privilege. My church is full of volunteers. It is easier to go through my church directory and count those who *do not help* in some way (and if you include those who have volunteered in the past the number is very small indeed). Looking around my congregations on a Sunday morning, I see a church that is active and working, the Body of Christ coming to worship.

Since volunteers are so important to the life of the church, it is vital that we treat them well. We should encourage, equip and support them. This is not just a practical imperative. It is a theological one. Both aspects will be explored in the following chapters.

This book is focused on volunteers within churches and the work they do. It looks at the issues that are most important for the 'average' church, so it is focused on the small scale and the local. It offers realistic suggestions and guidelines that do not rely on large budgets and staff, and is intensely practical and aims to cover the wide range of issues that will arise in the regular, day-to-day work of a church. It is about the intense and rewarding experience that working with volunteers entails.

It is also about working with volunteers in such a way that they can see just how important they are in the bigger picture of God's mission, well beyond the specific thing they are doing, however small and seemingly insignificant. There is a story of Christopher Wren visiting the site of the new St Paul's Cathedral. He was watching his design take shape when he noticed two workers labouring laying bricks in one of the walls. One of them seemed bored and laboured slowly, clearly not engaged in his work. The other was working hard, with great enthusiasm. Wren went up to the first bricklayer and asked him what he was doing. 'What does it look like?' he replied, 'I'm laying bricks!' Wren then went to the second and asked the same question, 'What are you doing?' The second bricklayer looked up and greeted Wren with a smile and a nod, 'I'm building a magnificent cathedral, sir.'

Do your volunteers have the bigger picture at the front of their minds when they are struggling to cut out the 13th fish to illustrate the miraculous catch or to stick the cotton wool on to yet another cardboard sheep? Such things, alongside the most extravagant act of service, are all small building blocks of the kingdom of God that he will take and use.

Leading volunteers well is about building up the Body of Christ to carry out the 'Great Commission' to 'go and make disciples of all nations' (see Matthew 28:16–20). That is the greatest vision possible. I hope this book will play a part in helping you do just that.

Chapter 1

Why people volunteer— and what it offers them in return

How big is volunteering?

The number of people involved in volunteering is very significant indeed. Research from 2008/09 records that 41 per cent of UK adults volunteered formally (giving unpaid help through a group, club or organisation) and 62 per cent informally (giving unpaid help as an individual to someone who is not a relative). A little over a third of these were involved in religious activities.[3] The monetary value of such help is significant too. In 2007/08 formal volunteers alone contributed an estimated £22.7 billion to the UK economy.[4] It is impossible to calculate the value of the informal sector, but think of how often you hear huge figures associated with the work of unpaid family carers.

Yet all in the garden of volunteering is not rosy. The average number of hours spent volunteering per volunteer declined by 30 per cent between 1997 and 2007. Although the actual number of volunteers increased across that period, it now seems to have plateaued.[5] Reports from many charities suggest that it is difficult to recruit new volunteers for regular, long-term projects, although there is more success for 'episodic' volunteering, for occasional or one-off events. The London 2012 Olympics, for example, had 70,000 volunteers working alongside the paid staff (and incidentally, it was generally agreed that they contributed significantly to that event's success). The many 'fun runs' and Comic Relief-type events that are organised show people's willingness to put themselves out for a cause.

One might expect that the churches would fare proportionally better but the evidence is mixed. The 2001 Citizenship Survey[6] suggests that faith as such does not make much difference to whether you are likely to volunteer or not, as the proportion of people volunteering who had a religious affiliation is similar to the proportion of people with none (although of the various faiths included, Christians were among the most likely to volunteer). The active *practice* of faith, however, does seem to make a considerable difference.[7]

Robert Putnam (Professor of International Peace at Harvard University) suggests there is 'robust... scientific evidence' to show that having faith makes people better citizens. 'By many different measures, religious people are better friends, better neighbours, better citizens, than non-religious people... [They are] two to three times more likely to work on community projects.'[8] There is a good relationship between the level of someone's prayer life and the time spent volunteering and also between church attendance and taking one's wider social responsibility seriously. This link is illustrated by the nfpSynergy[9] survey referred to above, which reports that 29 per cent of those who are regular worshippers had volunteered within the last three months, against 15 per cent for those who are not. Overall the scale of volunteering related to faith remains high. Religion is the fourth most important field for formal volunteering (23 per cent of all respondents), and for black and Asian people it represents by far the largest field of interest.[10] Recent research for the Church of England indicates that more people do unpaid work for church organisations than for any other group: eight per cent of all adults in the UK (which is around half of all those coming to church).[11]

Such volunteering is not just to keep the churches and their own organisations going. A quarter of regular churchgoers across all denominations are involved in voluntary community service outside the church. They contribute an amazing 23.2 million hours of voluntary service each month to their local communities. The Church of England, for example, provides activities outside church worship for 407,000 children and young people aged under 16 years, and 32,900 young people aged 16 to 25 years, with more than 116,000 volunteers helping out with these.

Looking at these figures, we can begin to see something of what volunteers bring to the church and wider community. Just take my own church as an illustration. Here are a few examples of what the members do beyond worship and church groups: support prison chaplaincy and asylum seekers, help with the local hospice and schools and a community café, work with Samaritans, the Scout and Guide Movement, sports coaching, cricket umpiring, lead walks and the local Alcoholics Anonymous group. Such examples 'flesh out' the bare figures.

This pattern is repeated time and again across most of the thousands of churches in this country. Christian service has never been just to members of their own church or faith. Church members naturally reach out to serve members of any faith group, or none.

Why do people volunteer?

There are a huge variety of reasons. People may share the vision for the project, a real passion for the particular cause or group, but that is by no means always the case. People can be just as easily drawn in by a friend and then develop a passion, or feel prompted by a personal need.

Here is a selection of some of the reasons for volunteering that have been given to me:

- Some people have a strong personal motivation:
  - 'There's no point in just grumbling, we can make a difference by doing things together.'

- Some have a personal commitment to the cause:
  - 'Our daughter suffers from epilepsy and we wanted to help others.'

- For others it is a more general concern for the community:
  - 'There is little for children to do around here. I can't just leave things to other people.'
  - 'The community needs something, and I want to be involved.'

- Sometimes it is through example:
  - 'I was conditioned into volunteering by schooling and by my parents.'
  - 'It all started with the Scouts.'

- Sometimes it is far more personal:
  - 'I need to feel I'm doing something worthwhile, that people need me.'
  - 'I want to make a difference.'

- It may even be a desire for company or friendship:
  - 'I need to get out of the house.'; 'I want to meet others.'

- For some, it may be to find fulfilment in life that other aspects do not satisfy:
  - 'I've worked in lousy jobs... minimum wage, poor hours... The nice thing about volunteering is to [work] in something you enjoy.'

- There may even be something a little more contractual about it for some:
  - 'I want to get my children into the CofE High School.'
  - 'I do it for the experience, for my CV.'

While not suggesting that this last one is a major factor, we should bear in mind that not all volunteering is totally altruistic. Then of course there is the classic reason—'The vicar asked me!'—which we will return to in Chapter 5.

All the above responses were given by churchgoers, although they are much the same kind of replies you would get by asking any group of volunteers. Many recognise, and are quite open about, the good that volunteering does to them, as well as the good done by them. There is a strong emotional side to volunteering.

For Christians there are additional spiritual drivers:

- 'I believe I am called to make a difference, to be salt and light.'
- 'I think of it more as serving than volunteering. As Christians we are led to serve. That's an important distinction.'
- 'A lot has been down to my faith.'
- 'If we have a faith, good things come out of it.'

Although that is not to say that such things as guilt do not figure here too:

- 'I feel I should. I have children, so I volunteer to help in Sunday school.'

This kind of response can develop in a way the person never realised. At a workshop on children's work the speaker mentioned he had run the crèche, then the Sunday school, then the youth group, each time moving up with his children. He wanted something available for his own children and was prepared to step forward. He is now an ordained minister.

Some people find that doing something quite different from their daily work can be very energising, so this is what they look for. Two of our bell-ringers have told me that an evening of ringing is an ideal antidote to work-based stress. Others are happy to use their gifts and work experience (but please, please, do not always expect teachers to do your children's work). The joy of volunteering is that it is exactly that—it is voluntary. It can offer quite different opportunities to other aspects of life, which is good for the individual, and good for the church.

Being aware of the variety of reasons is a good place to start in understanding the general motivation of the volunteers with whom you work. There are many resources available if you wish to look further into theories about motivation and how it works.[12] I refer to them here simply to stress the importance of remembering that reasons for volunteering are many and varied. We should never assume others are doing something for the same reasons we are, nor should we make assumptions as to why people do not volunteer.

We are facing the ageing of many key volunteers and greater difficulty recruiting their replacements. In order to maximise the number of volunteers you have to draw upon, it is important to think of reasons why people may not volunteer or why those who do may struggle to continue offering what they have in the past, as well as taking into account the changes in the way people are volunteering today.

At the beginning of this chapter I referred to the recent trend of the plateauing of numbers and the reduction in volunteer hours. We must not assume that the churches will be immune from such changes.

Why are people not volunteering as much as they used to?

There are many reasons contributing to this change.

We live in an increasingly busy and stressed society. Even our leisure time is far more organised than it used to be. The fact that so many people are 'money rich, time poor' is especially relevant since time is very much what voluntary organisations rely on. I have experience of this first hand. For nearly eight years I commuted into London every day. I left home before 7am and did not get back until a little after 7pm. I simply did not have a great deal of time to volunteer. In the past, meetings in my parish regularly went on until nearly 11pm. Now if we go much past 9.30pm a lot of people get twitchy! Ten pm (having started at 7.30pm) is an absolute deadline.

Family life is growing in complexity. There are now more two-income families with both parents working, and other time and economic pressures that prevent either parent being so available. The number of single parent families is growing, and with it issues of child care arrangements, visiting patterns among separated families, 'blended' families with four or more sets of grandparents, all of whom need to be visited.

There are other issues that might deter people from offering their time, such as the growing 'health and safety' culture (perhaps more media-driven than real, but a growing concern nonetheless), with its sapping of even reasonable risk-taking. Or the need for so much form-filling and training for child safeguarding, which a proportion of those who might otherwise volunteer find off-putting.

There is the significant fact that people simply no longer join things, from political parties to local drama clubs, in the numbers they used to do. Robert Putnam describes how people in America were becoming increasingly disconnected from family, friends and neighbours.[13] People no longer join clubs and teams but rather do more on their own. He warns that our stock of 'social capital', our connections with each other, has plummeted and that this has impoverished our lives and communities. As with many trends, this has crossed the Atlantic and now can also be seen in the UK. Membership of all sorts of organisations, including churches, has dropped. Interestingly, some of the more campaigning charities and some of those that offer something in return, such as the National Trust and RSPB, have seen their membership (although not necessarily volunteer numbers) increase.

Alongside the more negative or complicating factors, is a change in people's expectations. According to Jonathan and Thomas McKee in *The New Breed*,[14] volunteers today:

- want more flexibility
- expect to be empowered
- will not tolerate working alongside people who are incompetent
- are very 'tech savvy'
- do not want to be micromanaged
- want to make more than a contribution, they want to make a difference

Not only may people demand more from their volunteering today, but they may not have the history of volunteering that previous generations had to know exactly what volunteering entails and what it can offer. They may not have had the example of parents or friends who volunteer. Thinking in church terms, the Body functions properly only when *everyone* is playing their part. Individuals may need more encouragement to do so today.

We will explore issues around recruitment and retention in the following chapters. First we will consider some general issues facing all of us today, simply because of the shared culture in which we live. A whole variety of issues are more to do with the period in which we were born and how this affects the way we think and act, and in particular with regards to volunteering.

Chapter 2

Understanding today's volunteers

When we think of the Body of Christ, we usually link it with people's spiritual gifts and natural abilities. We also think of different types of personality, for example, those more upfront and those who prefer to stay in the background. We may consider the different ages of people, but only in so far as what they might be able to do and what we might need to provide for them. There is another whole area of study that has only come to the fore comparatively recently, that of generational theory. It is also helpful to think of the Body as made up of people of different generations, who exhibit characteristics related to each generation.

Those born in a certain period share many general attitudes to life, and these periods tend to change every 20 years or so.[15] Although there is not complete agreement on the precise point at which one generation becomes another (and these vary somewhat from country to country), the divisions for the UK are generally agreed to be (by date of birth):

- 1920s to 1945—'Silent Generation' (also 'Traditionalist' or 'Builder')
- 1945 to early 1960s—'Baby Boomer'
- mid 1960s to early 1980s—'Generation X' (also 'Busters' or 'MTV generation')

- mid 1980s to early 2000s—'Generation Y' (also known as 'Millennials' or 'Generation next', sometimes 'Echo Boomers' because of certain traits they have in common with 'Baby Boomers')

There is an earlier generation, the 'Greatest' or 'World War' generation, from 1901 to the mid 1920s, but as the youngest of those are now around 90, I propose to leave them to a well-deserved retirement. There is a later generation, which has yet to be named to general agreement (Generation Z is one very unimaginative one), but they are mostly too young to be involved in significant amounts of volunteering so far, and their characteristics have yet to emerge fully.

You could perhaps sum up the attitude of the different generations as follows:

- Silent Generation—commitment and duty
- Boomers—more selfish but still a large place for hard work and deferred gratification
- Gen X—'What suits me—now!'
- Gen Y—'Whatever!'

Stereotypical? Yes, but not a bad place to start. Let's explore the attitudes of each generation a little more and see how that might affect the way we need to treat them in order to get the best out of them and indeed to encourage them to volunteer for us at all. You might assume that a Christian commitment will make a significant difference. Not necessarily: 'I'm a Boomer; I go to church for what I can give. My younger friends, if it doesn't completely suit them, will simply leave.' Different generations, even when they share the same faith, can have very different perspectives.

As you read you may find that you fit some of your generation's characteristics but not all. That should not surprise you, as these are general patterns. You may also find that you share attitudes of more than one generation. This would not be surprising as those on the 'cusp', in other words, a few years either side of a generational change, often exhibit characteristics of both.

Silent Generation

Members of the Silent Generation have a very high self-motivation factor, allied to a high sense of duty and an assumption that they have to work for everything. That is hardly surprising as many experienced both the Depression Era and the Second World War, and the few that did not still went through very tough times economically in their childhood. They were also used to doing what those in authority told them.

They are generally conservative, hard-working (and expect others to be the same) and like structure and rules, order and formal hierarchies. They like to know where they stand in an organisation. They have a 'waste not, want not' mentality and a real fear of getting into debt. It is often a matter of pride to pay bills as they come. They are generally frugal and save every penny where they can. Even though they may have considerable savings, they are often very reluctant to spend. It is far more likely to be older Boomers than the Silent Generation who are members of the SKI set ('Spending the Kids' Inheritance'). Some, though, having worked hard all their lives, are at last learning to relax. They are taking world cruises and other long-haul holidays while their health holds out. They are exemplars of the phrase 'deferred gratification'.

They are loyal and dedicated, often having given their life to church as the main outlet for their time and social life outside of work. And they often continue to show great dedication, well above and beyond the call of duty. A couple in my church split their time between here and Madeira, being involved with churches in both locations. Recently the husband, who was the church council secretary, flew back from the UK to take notes for a meeting—at his own expense!

Many women of the Silent Generation never worked after marriage or certainly not after they had children. They had time to give and time to socialise, without too much pressure. Look around your various groups. How many of the female volunteers who are now in their 70s have been helping in one capacity or another for most of their lives? And how many continue to provide a good deal of the pastoral care for others who are even more elderly, running the women's and senior citizens' groups?

The younger members of this generation, as with older Boomers, are having more and more of their time absorbed by caring for grandchildren,[16] as the next generation tends to have two working parents. They are also enjoying the freedom that their good pensions allow them for frequent holidays, and both of these factors are making a regular commitment more difficult.

Baby Boomers

This is the generation who discovered consumerism, brands and new freedoms. They are used to choice, but the amount of choice these days is beginning to tax them. They may well be loyal to a church in the same way they would be to their bank or make of car, but the loyalty is not as strong as that of the previous generation. If any of these no longer offer the same 'quality' or 'reliability', they will change. Equally they are no longer used to staying with one employer throughout their working life, and so also may wish to change the areas in which they volunteer from time to time, in order to develop their interests and skills. They appreciate a 'menu' of opportunities, both shorter and longer term, that they can fit around their lifestyles. They are often happy to give time, but they want more self-satisfaction from what they give than the previous generation did. They are old enough to know what they want and what they do not want from life, and that includes volunteering.

According to research, volunteering currently peaks in mid-life, then declines. Thus it is the Boomers that, at present, form the bulk of volunteers.[17] This is likely to remain the case for some years to come, although many Gen Xers are already stepping into their shoes. There are other Boomers, at or approaching retirement, who have lots of skills and experience but are not used to volunteering. They are a good target group as they may well wish to give something back to the society that has given them so much.

Boomers are currently the most powerful generation in many ways, in terms of spending power and simply through being in numerous positions of leadership in business, politics and church. They grew up in a time of rapid social change, becoming the first teenagers and the founder members of the counterculture. They became more politically aware at a younger age than the previous generation. They may now be reconnecting to their youthful desire to make a difference, which they were not able to do for decades because of the constraints of work.

When they retire, they are in no hurry to 'retire' completely as they know they are likely to have 15 or more active years ahead of them. When Paul McCartney wrote 'When I'm 64', the average life expectancy was around 67 years for a man and 74 for a woman. Now it is around 78 for a man and 82 for a woman, and increasing all the time. Some people are claiming that 60 is the new 50, if not the new 40, and 70 the new 50. The Rolling Stones continue to play to packed concerts in their 60s, Cliff Richard (a cusp Silent Generation/Boomer) in his 70s. They don't think of themselves as old. As a younger Boomer myself I have little interest as yet in Saga holidays, tea dances or bingo!

While I was working for CMS in the late 1990s and early years of the current millennium, we began to notice a new trend. People were retiring who had huge amounts of energy and many skills to offer. Up until that point we had, like many organisations, a 'Gap Year' programme. Now we developed such a programme for retiring Boomers (or cusp Boomers at that time). Once it was running we found lots of advantages—such people would happily stay for two or three years, or more, not just the inside of one. They had far more skills and life experience to offer.

Boomers may not automatically look for opportunities to give their newly found time, although some do.[18] A friend of mine who retired a few years ago said that he planned to divide his week into three. One third was for continuing to earn money (perhaps not necessary for those Boomers with particularly good pensions), one third for himself and his family and one third for volunteering. If only a proportion of that generation think similarly, and my experience is that they do, then that will result in a lot of potential volunteering time. (After all, they are not called the 'Baby Boomers' for nothing—there are a lot of them.)

As a whole they are the first, and the last, generation to be affluent in retirement. Many have more than adequate money and spare time, although some may be asset rich and cash poor. They have a greater opportunity to fulfil their expectations, although this is getting less so for the members of the generation still to retire as the current economic crisis continues.

Younger Boomers and older Gen X parents may not yet have grandparenting issues but a lot of them are 'helicopter parents' (always flying in with resources to help sort out their offspring's problems). This affects them time-wise but also affects their now-adult children; so that Gen Y in particular are less confident without advice and supervision. They may even have children still at home while, at the same time, be caring for elderly parents. This further constrains their time and makes commitment more difficult. This is the first generation where this combination is a common factor.

Generation X

A highly significant factor for this and the subsequent generations is the influence of technology, the speed of change and ease of access to information. They are comfortable with this and quite frustrated when others in the previous generations do not have the same enthusiasm—'What do you mean, you're not on email?' They will not believe something simply because they have been told. They will not do something simply because that is the way it has always been done.

Their time is precious and they do not like it wasted. Both sexes may have to fit volunteering around a full-time job and caring for a family, as both partners now have the expectation that the man will take a full part in family life. This means they will need more options and flexibility in volunteering. And they love change, so much so that they actually need it. Take holidays, for example: the Silent Generation are likely to have one or two favourite places, usually in the UK. Older Boomers will have a few more, and more often abroad. For younger Boomers and Gen X it is more likely to be a different holiday destination each time.

They are much less tolerant of poorly led meetings or sloppily planned activities. A phrase that has grown up around this generation is, 'It must fit me exactly', and that relates to much more than clothes and the colours of their walls. If what we offer (in terms of volunteering but also in terms of worship and activities) does not 'fit' them, they are likely to be quick to take their precious skills, time and money elsewhere. Loyalty, whether to their bank, utility company, political party or church, is no longer an overriding factor but depends on such things as level of service and value for money.

Gen X volunteers will expect to be consulted about the work far more than the previous generations. They believe their views count, and they are suspicious of assumed expertise in others. If they are not consulted, they are likely to react against decisions, not necessarily because they disagree but simply because their opinions were not asked for. They also dislike close supervision. They want to be trusted to get on with the job, not have someone always looking over their shoulder, even if only metaphorically.

The five principles of a group of young (mid-20s to mid-

30s) social entrepreneurs—the 'Pioneers of Change'[19]—are: Be yourself; Do what matters; Start now; Engage with others; Never stop asking. That could almost be seen as a manifesto for younger Gen X and older Gen Y. If that is true, it bodes well for encouraging volunteering, since altruism and making a difference in life are key characteristics for this group.

Yet, when combined with their work patterns and other commitments, it is easier to find volunteers from this generation for one-off 'special' events or rallies for a cause than helping at regular week-by-week activities, which give them less of a buzz. 'Comic Relief'-type events are popular as they also involve having fun. Such events are one way of connecting people to other volunteer opportunities, enabling them to see the joy and pleasure of volunteering and getting a taste for it. This may lead to more committed and long-term volunteering in the future when, of course, their lifestyle is more likely to allow this.

Generation Y

Whereas Gen X have come to make great use of technology, Gen Y are the 'digital natives'. They have been brought up surrounded by the technology which they not only use to gain information but, to a great extent, through which they live their lives. Everything is instant; huge amounts of personal information is shared and thus they have a very high expectation of personal sharing in return. This is the socially networked generation, and it shows in volunteering.

Video gaming, on computers, consoles, smartphones and tablets, is not only all-pervasive but leads to a desire to keep 'working up'. They are always keen to get to the next level, where they know the game will be harder but the rewards greater. They are great multitaskers and generally 'consume' more than one medium at once. Our 23-year-old son listens to 20 hours of podcasts a week, often while playing a game, watching a DVD, updating his Facebook status, tweeting or even reading. They are used to processing information differently, from multiple, networked sources (the whole basis of the internet), not sequentially as in a book or even an old-fashioned video. This can lead to some distinctly different behaviours. For example, if they use their smartphone in a meeting, it does not mean they are not concentrating, but they may be accessing some relevant information, making notes, or doing a number of other things. They might, of course, be playing a game or tweeting comments.

Sometimes described as 'Gen X on steroids', Gen Y and especially volunteers of that age group will expect a more intense reaction more immediately than previous generations. To be successful, a project will have to provide perks like community, fun, enjoyment and have a high 'take home value'. They like to know what is expected of them and feel most comfortable in areas they know they can do well. They also may do things as a volunteer in different ways to those you have used in the past. Rather than try and squeeze them into existing moulds, ask yourself, 'If it gets the job done, does it matter?'

Even more than Gen X, Gen Y like to know where they stand. When leading and encouraging those of this generation, we must make it clear that they can say 'no' to any further commitment if they wish; that when they take on a job it isn't for 'life' but it can be handed over. If people feel 'locked in', they might simply leave rather than try to renegotiate. It may be inconvenient when people say 'no'. It may mean valuable work will have to stop, but without such a 'contract' you are less likely to recruit from this generation in the first place, and certainly less likely to see the group flourishing.

Gen Y are also, according to James Lawrence, 'the experience generation. How they feel about something is as important as what they think'.[20] If Gen X expect to be consulted, Gen Y expect to be right in there with the decision-making. Gen Y really want a group with which to volunteer, and they love working with others in a close-knit team. Be wary of asking them to do anything on their own. So, if your church does decide to run internships, it is best for this to be a group, not an individual, experience.

They expect choice in everything (how many models of mobile phone are on the market; how many brands of tea on a supermarket shelf?), and are well used to exercising that choice. If your group or church cannot offer what they want, they will look for another. Even if they do 'sign up', they will expect more reminding than previous generations. For a generation that plans via text and Facebook rather than diaries and notes, communication becomes a high priority, including last minute communication.

Interestingly, when I started doing the research for this project, I found that some younger leaders were themselves finding it a struggle to get others of their generation to take on leadership roles. The potential leaders were competent; they had plenty of confidence; it was just that they preferred being part of a team with someone else taking on the organising and detailed planning. One Gen Y leader put it this way: 'The culture among young people is that when they ask "Can I help?", they mean "Can I turn up whenever I want?"' This brings lots of practical difficulties in its wake. It is difficult to manage the project, sort out rotas, and so on. For many in this generation volunteering is an extra, an add-on. They look for their satisfaction elsewhere—some from work, quite a lot from leisure, for example games, nights out and social networking. They work to a more flexible, 'on the spur of the moment' timetable, rather than the more regular pattern of previous generations.

That is, if you have members of that generation among your volunteers at all. In the last few years people have become acutely aware of the effect of the current education/employment situation on the younger members of Gen Y. It is not just about whether young people want to volunteer. It is also about whether they can afford to volunteer at all. If they do, they volunteer in a different way from previous generations. They volunteer more often for one-off or short-term projects, not for life. Within the church you might look to something like the 'Soul in the City' and 'Hope' initiatives (or our very own local equivalent, Love Huddersfield)—short-term events with an emphasis on witness through practical service.

Recent holiday clubs at my church have seen a good number of Gen Y, but the regular youth work of the church is still done mainly by older Gen X and Boomers (with the occasional Silent Generation member too). The passion is still there, but it is expressed differently. Gap year volunteering is increasingly popular, but only a small proportion of those taking part are likely to go on straight away to become regular volunteers with that organisation. They may come back years later for another one-off project, and years later again for a more regular involvement. Time will tell.

Generation to generation

This is just a snapshot. There is plenty of material available to explore this further. I hope it illustrates some of the differences in the way you may have to treat volunteers of younger generations compared to the way the church treated them in the past (and perhaps the way you yourself were treated in the past). These characteristics come into play in all sorts of areas—recruiting, the way they work in teams, how they wish to be supported, how they respond to tensions and conflicts. Indeed it would be good to keep these characteristics in your mind in pretty much every area we go on to explore in this book.

There can be tensions between the generations. The *British Attitudes Survey* of 2010[21] reports that the young are more likely to feel discriminated against, and are viewed more negatively than the elderly by others; that people in Britain are generally more positive about old people than young people and that older people feel more negatively towards the young than they do about others in their own generation. Not always the best dynamics for a mixed-age team! Boomers tend to criticise Gen X for being lazy, working to their own schedules, selfish, not dependable, and so on.[22] Interestingly, comments between Gen X and Gen Y can be very similar. In one church a Gen X leader, who had recently completed several years of training for a volunteer ministry, decided to move to a nearby church in a different denomination. For them the move was completely logical as it fitted their needs and lifestyle better. For those of the Silent Generation left behind it was a betrayal, a dereliction of duty, showing a lack of commitment.

Different generational emphases will mean more complex team dynamics. In some ways there is nothing new in all this, there always seems to have been a certain amount of antagonism between generations. In 1 Timothy Paul is in one moment encouraging Timothy in the face of criticism from his elders: 'Don't let anyone look down on you because you are young' (1 Timothy 4:12) and only a few verses later reminding him not to 'rebuke an older man harshly' (5:1–2). Perhaps there is something here of the way the young have always looked at the old, and vice versa. Let us be honest: might not those of us of the Boomer and Silent Generations just *occasionally* feel like being a bit more demanding, a little more self-centred? And would not the flexibility and extra input required to be invested in Gen X and Y volunteers give returns if used with the older generations too, those whose dedication we have perhaps for too long taken for granted?

I wonder whether we need to add some more couplets into Paul's list in Galatians 3:28: 'neither Babyboomers nor Gen X, Silent Generation or Gen Y...'? Whatever the differences, we are all made in God's image, and all have our place in the Body of Christ. As a leader I am called to love those who are like me and those who are very different from me; those who play by my rules and those who do not; those whose actions hurt others, as well as those they hurt. I suspect Paul struggled to love Mark (a much younger man) after he had let him down (Acts 15:36–41). Yet later he saw him as a valued colleague (Colossians 4:10; 2 Timothy 4:11). Paul was living out his own teachings in 1 Corinthians 13:5

by not being 'easily angered' and keeping 'no record of wrongs'.

Before this starts sounding too much like hard work, it is worth looking back at the attributes of the different generations and see what teams with a mix of ages might be like. Matching the commitment of the older generations to the energy, knowledge and application of the younger can lead to a lot of dynamism. Teams benefit greatly from including different generations as well as a wide variety of individuals. I would also suggest the importance of mixing up ages in teams for another reason. When people work alongside each other, prejudices and stereotypical thinking tend to make way for deep and lasting friendships and mutual respect.

Each one an individual

In all this talk of trends and generalities let us not forget that people are individuals and thus have individual differences too. The broad brush approach is useful for awareness, for seeing where potential benefits and problems may lie, but there is nothing to match good knowledge of each and every individual in your team. I do not say 'church' as, unless your church is a very small one, that would be impossible. In a larger church you need to rely on other leaders for this awareness.

Whether knowledge is broad brush or of individual differences, the development and leadership of volunteers needs to adapt to the current climate. Of whatever generation they are, people may not have so much time to give today as they did in the past. They want to see meetings well organised and focused on the outcomes. There is a fear of meetings eating up time unproductively, and people do not have the time to 'waste' any more. How many meetings do we take part in that could be run far more effectively? People today want to talk less and do more. They want to work *with* rather than *under*. They are far less willing to put up with poor performance and also want to have their voices heard more.

And there is more 'competition' among organisations. If you cannot provide what volunteers need, they may well move on to somewhere that can. We cannot afford to be unprofessional with the 'time poor' volunteers we have today as the Body is increasingly busy.

Chapter 3

Building up the Body of Christ

For we were all baptised by one Spirit so as to form one body.
1 CORINTHIANS 12:13

The Body is a given: that is what we are. But what makes *the* Body different from any other body of people? There are many ways this theme could be developed, but I am limiting myself here to how it relates to the way we do our work. It is clear from the statistics in our opening chapter, and simply from looking around us, that many who do not share our faith (or indeed any faith) still spend themselves in the service of others. Many do so in dedicated ways that challenge those of us who claim to follow a Servant Lord. It is good to remind ourselves just why our faith makes service such a central part.

I have found it fascinating to explore a theology of volunteering. Since 'you are not your own; you were bought at a price' (1 Corinthians 6:19–20), perhaps we just have to assume that we ought to use all we have for God. Having said that, we should note that this verse comes in the middle of a section on sexual immorality and so is not the best place to start for a more general exposition. The only place I can find volunteering specifically mentioned is in 1 Corinthians 9:17: 'If I preach voluntarily, I have a reward', yet in the same chapter Paul argues that receiving payment for ministry is fine too.

I would begin with the call of Jesus to the disciples (Matthew 4:19; Mark 1:17) and to the rich young man (Luke 18:22): 'Come, follow me.' All that God calls us to is voluntary. He *invites* us to become his disciples; he *asks* us to live for him; he *encourages* us to serve others as he served others.

From the earliest days Christians have been encouraged 'to remember the poor' (Galatians 2:10) or 'look after widows and orphans' (James 1:27) as a key outworking of their faith. This is clearly more than just giving money. Indeed James is a good place to look for all sorts of practical outworking of our faith as in chapter 2 comes the often quoted 'faith... [without] action, is dead' (v. 17). Such an encouragement to do 'good deeds' comes not just in James, though, but in the great majority of the New Testament authors:

'Let your light shine before others, that they may see your good deeds and glorify your Father in heaven.' (Matthew 5:16)

'Never tire of doing what is good.' (2 Thessalonians 3:13)

'Command them to do good, to be rich in good deeds.' (1 Timothy 6:18)

'Those who have trusted in God may be careful to devote themselves to doing what is good.' (Titus 3:8)

'Let us consider how we may spur one another on towards love and good deeds.' (Hebrews 10:24)

'You should use whatever gift you have received to serve others.' (1 Peter 4:10)

Look at the language. Each of the writers is clear what is to be done. But, with the exception of Paul (never one to mince his words), the language is conditional, persuasive, not commanding.

Philippians 2:3–4 encourages us not to look to our 'own interests but... to the interests of the others'. That comes before and goes far beyond formal volunteering. Recently our church has been made aware of the needs of asylum seekers, particularly those going through the appeal process after having their initial claim rejected. Such people have no access to financial or housing support of any kind and we were concerned about this. We looked at what we might do as a church that went beyond giving money or signing petitions. This has led to several members of the church becoming hosts, offering accommodation, food and other forms of support.

We follow the One who came 'not to be served, but to serve' (Matthew 20:26–28; Mark 10:42–45), and we see Jesus serving time and again. Does this have any limits? There is little in the Gospels about the disciples 'chilling' (the Gospel writers did not waste valuable space on what they considered hardly an important thing). Yet in Mark 6 Jesus and his disciples were having a particularly busy time, and Jesus told them to 'come with me by yourselves to a quiet place and get some rest' (v. 31). Just a short while later, though, he ended up first teaching and then feeding a vast crowd. He put his own needs second and got stuck in once again. That is not to be interpreted as a recipe for burnout, however. Jesus did not spend all his time healing and teaching (Luke 5:15–16). We can assume that as a perfect example of humanity he managed to achieve the perfect work/non-work balance in his life.[23]

In Mark 8:34–38 we are told we 'must deny [our]selves...' When we look at this verse we tend to concentrate more on the continuation—'take up your cross'. This follows a passage in which Jesus has said that he will literally give his life for his mission, yet that is a one-off, the ultimate step. This passage more generally calls us to radical discipleship, spending ourselves in whatever our commitment to Jesus entails. That surely includes spending oneself in the service of others.

In Matthew 25:31–46 we see a further call to a variety of forms of service. It is clear from this that, not only is service of others the right thing to do in itself, but in doing so you are serving Jesus himself (v. 40). It also has the more chilling sequel for those who have not done such acts of service—'Depart from me, you who are cursed...' (v. 41). Some people interpret this passage as encouraging caring actions only towards fellow Christians—'the least of these brothers and sisters of mine' (v. 40). I would argue strongly that this is meant more generally, that we meet Jesus in all those in need. In either case we are called to do more than merely say, 'Go in peace; keep warm and well fed' (James 2:16).

We tend to interpret verses such as 1 Corinthians 15:58—'Always give yourselves fully to the work of the Lord, because you know that your labour in the Lord is not in vain'—in terms of 'spiritual' labour, but I do not think it can be limited to that. It comes after the long excursion on the Body and gifts earlier in that letter, with the great passage about love in the middle, and it is followed by a request to take a collection for others' needs, and some personal requests from Paul asking that they 'help [him] on [his] journey' (16:6). It also follows after the passage of confidence in eternal life in chapter 15. It is because of this promise that what we do is not 'in vain' (vv. 2, 58). God's promises, God's perspective, what God offers beyond this life makes it so important that we give our lives for him, and thus for others, in this life.

To be a true 'amateur' means to learn about and follow best practice, to prepare as well as we can, to work as hard as we can, because we should do everything as if 'working for the Lord, not for human masters' (Colossians 3: 23).

Hebrews 13:16 says, 'And do not forget to do good and to share with others, for with such sacrifices God is pleased'. Sharing is a voluntary thing—giving of what you have that others do not. From a human perspective, they do not have a right to expect such sharing of time, possessions or money—yet sharing like this is seen as part of our service to God. It might be at a sacrificial level, because that is the kind of life we should be leading. As with 1 Corinthians 15:58, the passage in Hebrews also comes after the long theological discourse and at the beginning of the practical section. As in so many of Paul's letters he begins by saying what we should believe and follows this by telling us what those beliefs should drive us to do. Paul led by example; he was driven to serve sacrificially: 'So, I will very gladly spend for you everything I have and expend myself as well' (2 Corinthians 12:15).

We are called to work with God to bring his kingdom and its values into play. That is our outward reference, and there is an internal one too. If we believe that faith must be lived out, that people are built up through service, then we should expect to see people growing in faith through serving others. John says, 'It gave me great joy when some believers came and testified about your faithfulness to the truth' (3 John 1:3), which includes practical caring: 'you are faithful in what you are doing for the brothers and sisters, even though they are strangers to you' (v. 5). On this occasion he is referring to fellow believers, but that does not detract from the more general point. Paul makes the same point about the importance of carrying 'each other's burdens'— a totally voluntary experience—in order that we 'fulfil the law of Christ' (Galatians 6:2). The message of how faith becomes real through actions goes well beyond the letter of James.

Volunteering against the grain

As a small aside, the practical expression of our faith includes serving those whom we do not necessarily like and who may not like us: 'If you do good to those who are good to you, what credit is that to you?' (Luke 6:33). Bear that in mind when you have just had a mouthful of abuse from a homeless person you have tried to help! Romans 12:20, where Paul quotes Proverbs 25:21–22 about doing good to those who do you harm, is relevant here too. This is a powerful form of witness, and would certainly begin to draw out the difference of volunteering from a Christian perspective.

Spiritual gifts

This is often where we start when we come to think of Christian service within the Body. I have left it until last because the range of voluntary tasks on offer goes well beyond what we describe as 'spiritual' gifts, as important as these are.

There are four lists of spiritual gifts, although the first three passages are seen as the 'classic' ones:

1. Romans 12:3–8 (and there are some other related thoughts about the way we should act in the rest of the chapter)
2. 1 Corinthians 12:4–11, 28–30 (with an introduction before, in verses 2–3 and a section on the Body in between, in verses 12–27)
3. Ephesians 4:11 (with more on the Body before, in verses 3–7 and after, in verses 12–16)
4. 1 Peter 4:9–11

I propose to look only briefly at the 'practical' gifts from this list, as illustrated in action elsewhere in the New Testament, because these are the ones most relevant to the volunteering most of us do. Not that I do not think 'leadership' is practical, but I devote a whole chapter to this later.

So we have:

- Administration: the seven 'deacons' (Acts 6:1–7); appointing elders (Titus 1:5)
- Pastor: the 'overseer' taking care of the church (1 Timothy 3:1–7); the elders (1 Peter 5:1–4)
- Helps: the women who supported Jesus (Mark 15:40–41; Luke 8:2–3); Tabitha (Acts 9:36); Onesiphorus (2 Timothy 1:16–18). This links closely with the next gift, Service, which is seen more generally, including in most of the above, and in the life of Jesus himself. Some make much of the differentiation between

helping and serving, but I cannot see that this is particularly useful.

- Mercy: Jesus himself (Matthew 20:29–34); the 'sheep' (Matthew 25:31–40); illustrated by the Good Samaritan (Luke 10:33–35)
- Teaching: Jesus himself (for example, Matthew 7:28–29; Luke 4:32); Paul, Philip, Barnabas and more
- Hospitality: Lydia (Acts 16:14–15); Gaius (Romans 16:23)

Although many of the names in the list above are well known, others are not. Who remembers the other five deacons apart from Stephen and Philip? These gifts, with the exception of teaching, are very much 'out of the limelight' gifts, relating to the unsung work of many volunteers.

A key part of ministry is helping people to discover their gifts and where to exercise them.

When we did this in the church where I was a curate it led to one of the most powerful pastoral experiences I have ever had. We set out to identify everyone's top three gifts—yes, every single member of the congregation. I do not know if everyone has that many gifts but it is worth exploring, as you might just be surprised. We achieved this by each staff member, lay minister and church council member interviewing two or three church members (starting with each other). One of the people I was allocated was Ethel.

Every church needs an Ethel. She is there, wind, rain or shine, to open up. She is there to give out books and to collect them in. She tidies up around the place. She makes the tea and serves it with a smile. The church, and the opportunities it gives her to serve, is her life. I shall never forget the look on her face when I told her that I thought her gifts were hospitality, serving and encouragement. I said she was one of the people I most enjoyed seeing, someone who always put a smile on my face. She positively glowed. As someone who had never done well at school and was generally seen as part of the furniture (and a piece you often tripped over at that), she was not used to praise.

Ethel was already using her gifts but did not realise it. There will be people in your congregation who do not even realise they have a single spiritual gift that could be used for the benefit of others, and to build up the wider Body.

The Body in good SHAPE

As the New Living Translation puts it: 'In his grace, God has given us different gifts for doing certain things well' (Romans 12:6). There are many books and study guides on understanding and exploring spiritual gifts as a church, but I want to focus on just one, which sets them in a wider context. Over 20 years ago Rick Warren devised the SHAPE concept: **S**piritual gifts, **H**eart, **A**bilities, **P**ersonality and **E**xperiences. This has been developed into a really helpful workbook by another Saddleback Pastor, Erik Rees.[24] In summary this explores:

- **Spiritual Gifts:** a set of special abilities that God has given to you to share his love and serve others.
- **Heart:** the special passions God has given you so that you can glorify him on earth.
- **Abilities:** the set of talents that God gave you when you were born, and which he wants you to use to make an impact for him.
- **Personality:** the special way God wired you to navigate life and fulfil your unique kingdom purpose.
- **Experiences:** those parts of your past, both positive and painful, which God intends to use in great ways.

Working through this book is helpful, whether you think you know your gifts well or are not sure. It does not look at the gifts in isolation but as part of the whole person you are. An exercise like this is really useful in helping volunteers to work out the areas for which they might be best suited. Although it is good to encourage people to move outside their comfort zones at times, it is best not to 'encourage' them, and certainly not to 'twist arms', to do things that do not make a good fit for them. It is not good for them and not good for those being served. Looking at all five areas together can help you see that, although one or more of the areas seems to 'tick a box' for someone, taking them as a whole might suggest otherwise.

A person had a real passion for work with older people, but they felt she talked down to them and organised activities that fitted her own interests and likes more than theirs. After a while she became discouraged and left because of, as she put it, 'the lack of response'. That is hardly surprising. She had a passion but not the experience or abilities required.

I am keen on the SHAPE approach for another reason. It looks at all the positives in whatever personality type you are and does not divide types into 'good' and not so good. All of us will have our unique gifts and our unique shortcomings. The person mentioned above was able to find other areas of service that fitted her experience, personality and abilities. She just needed a little more help in identifying them.

'If the eye should say...'

'Just as a body, though one, has many parts… all its many parts form one body' (1 Corinthians 12:12)—and all those parts are different. The passage goes on to describe the foolishness of one part thinking it was not part of the Body because it was not like another. Equally foolish is one part thinking it *is* like another, when it patently is not. SHAPE links the spiritual drive and the practical issues, and sometimes the latter has to take precedence. For example, it is no use appointing a church treasurer who is no good with figures and has a phobia of spreadsheets.

As a visiting preacher one Sunday, I was seated with the choir.

The gentleman next to me was singing enthusiastically, lustily, with clear enjoyment—and distinctly off-key!

He was in his early 80s and had been a choir member since his childhood. Whether he had been singing off-key all that time I do not know. I hope not but, from experience elsewhere, I suspect he may well have been. And even if he had not, what was he contributing to the Body at that time? What must this have meant to the motivation of the other choir members? To their overall performance, and the worshipping congregation? 'If one part suffers, every part suffers with it' (v. 26), and I am sure some part of that particular Body was suffering! I certainly was. And what did it mean for the man himself? Even if he never found out his singing was not contributing to a harmonious whole, was he really building himself and others up? Is it valuing a person, is it truly loving, is it kind, to have them spend a good chunk of their life thinking they were doing something of value, when they should have been encouraged to do something else? I return to this delicate topic in Chapter 11.

Within the Body, all people, all passions, all abilities and experience can be used as all are valuable. But we need to make sure they are being used in the right place and in the right way. We each bring a strength where others are weak, we bring insights where others do not know where to start. Equally, others bring these for us. We need to be honest about our own strengths and limitations, and help others to be the same about theirs.

Spiritual fruit

Before thinking about specific gifts, we need to ensure that, whatever we do, we do it full of the 'fruit of the Spirit': 'love, joy, peace, forbearance, kindness, goodness, faithfulness, gentleness and self-control' (Galatians 5:22–23). While you may not be able to build these into any specific kind of role description, you can certainly encourage and model them.

Then, 'speaking the truth in love, we will grow to become in every respect the mature body of him who is the head, that is, Christ. From him the whole body, joined and held together by every supporting ligament, grows and builds itself up in love, as each part does its work' (Ephesians 4:15–16).

Chapter 4

Wider ways of volunteering

You may have a picture of your ideal volunteer: probably young to middle-aged, with average or better abilities, and certainly an existing member of your church. I want to suggest you look at volunteering and who might be your volunteers in a wider way, starting with those who are not there at all.

Virtual volunteering

With the rise of computer technology and the internet, there is a whole new area of volunteering that has only been possible since the beginning of the 21st century, offering a great deal of scope for specialised help. For example, I am involved with a community group whose logo was designed by someone who lived in Australia with no more difficulty than if they had lived down the road.

What could virtual volunteers do for you?

- **Website:** not just the design and construction but keeping it up to date. How about putting up transcripts or audio files of the sermons, photos of church events? (Bear in mind that you need permission from parents or carers before using photographs of children.) What about making a podcast, for example of a 'thought for the week'?

- **Social networking sites:** this is just the kind of thing that younger people can do for you, because the web is their natural environment. It makes no difference where in the world the administrator for your church Facebook page or moderator for your blog actually lives. It is not just about the technicalities, but also about thinking in the right way. What is worth putting up on Facebook? What should you Tweet about? There are clearly some 'do's and don't's' about this kind of web presence, as regular stories in the media make clear.[25]

- **Answering questions:** in the early days of the internet a group of volunteers from one of the Church of England's training colleges managed a Christian 'Question and Answer' site. Finding the right person to do something like this is a matter of careful selection and judgment. If someone suitable is out there blogging already, why not encourage them to blog with a bit more purpose?

- **Research:** how often have you wanted to know more about a topic or needed some facts and figures but have not known where to start looking for them? This is a great job for a virtual volunteer, as it can be done at their own convenience and, if they have the right gifts and interests, then it is a job they are likely to enjoy. It does not have to be a younger person. It could easily be a 'silver surfer' (an person over 50 using the internet regularly) as their numbers are growing fast. Perhaps you could ask several people to keep an eye out for news on topics of particular interest. A couple of my church members regularly send me notification on anything that pops up on eBay that relates to our church and community, so I have a chance of augmenting our archives with such things as old postcards and a family Bible. Talking of eBay...

- **Running an eBay site for the church:** setting up such a site is not difficult but it needs someone to run it. This job is not completely 'virtual' as it involves physical activities such as collection, photographing, wrapping and posting of items, but those functions could easily be split.

- **Church newsletter:** are you stuck for an editorial team in your church? Why not see if you can find someone a little further afield? As magazines are put together on the computer these days (and if yours is not, then you definitely need to look for a new volunteer for this job!), such a person does not have to be local. Our community newsletter is now being designed and laid out by someone thousands of miles away, liaising with a local editor. Proofreading is also something that can be done at a distance.
- **Notices:** to augment our written and spoken notices, we have recently introduced a rolling series of slides projected before and after services. If you do not have someone to produce those locally, look elsewhere.
- **News releases:** it is good if you have someone locally to do this but, providing you can have the right amount of contact with someone, it does not matter whether they are next door or in another country.
- **Digitising archives:** this is more a 'semi-virtual' role, as you would need access to the original documents (although photographs could be sent to someone for further work). We have had a volunteer who has digitised our entire burial records and produced a spreadsheet of our graveyard, with photographs and transcribed inscriptions. This is a good example of someone's personal passion meshing with a job that may not have been urgent but has been very useful for the many people who visit our church to research family history. What might your church have that is worth preserving in this way? Do you have many old photographs or slides that need scanning? All this could be done by a 'virtual' volunteer.
- **Crowdsourcing:** having a single volunteer doing much work is exceptional, so you could have many people doing a small amount each. Wikipedia is the best known example of a project being completed by many people, but the principle can be used for other projects.

- **Advocates**: are there certain issues on which you want to bring pressure to bear? In the past you might have asked people to write letters for you or to stuff envelopes. This can all now be done through email. The right person who gets interested is likely to find new avenues to explore as well.
- **Advice (consultancy)**: one of my own volunteering roles is with a small publishing group that offers a series of 'bite-sized' publications on a range of topics. The whole project can run only because of the many people who volunteer to be part of the editorial groups. Our group also has a 'wider fringe' of people who cannot get to the meetings but are happy to offer advice or other help as they can, providing it is through email or the occasional phone call.
- **Database design**: although there are commercial packages out there, you might want something simpler. A keen amateur who knows the package you use could be just the contact you need.
- **Keep in touch**: do you have students who have gone to college from your church, people who have gone abroad for short-term work, or even members who have moved away and would like to keep in touch? Someone with a heart for people and access to a computer could be your link. Not only can they express the church's ongoing concern for the person who is away but they can feed back prayer requests to the wider church. How about some 'virtual visiting' of those who can no longer get to church but have a phone or access to the internet? This is certainly not a replacement for actual face-to-face visits, but it can be a great addition and a really positive boost to someone's day.
- **Internet shopping**: this is something else that could be done for those do not have internet access for themselves or are less confident in using it. This area obviously brings up considerable issues of trust, with payments being made, but it is only a new variant on the same issues that have always been there in the 'real' world.

- **Translating:** this is unlikely to be a day-to-day need but I once wanted a prayer in Czech for a wedding. There are free websites you can use but, having tried one or two, I have my doubts as to their fluency. How about putting out a request across the internet?

Be creative with your ideas.[26]

Recruiting such volunteers may not be easy, but you do not personally have to recruit them any more than you do the local ones. The person in Australia who designed the logo for our community group was the son of another volunteer. If you don't know someone yourself, try asking your other volunteers. Those working with you are likely to be the best recruiters, whether for local or 'virtual' volunteers. As you might expect, there are also specialist websites.[27]

Involving all abilities

Volunteering can be a great way of involving people with a wide range of disabilities. An Australian campaign for raising awareness of the rights of people with disabilities used the strapline: 'Don't judge what I can do by what you think I can't.'

Someone who is registered blind is a keen and talented member of our bell-ringing team (with his guide dog at his feet). He has also just been elected as church warden. A middle-aged woman with special educational needs is an enthusiastic and caring member of our Sunday club team. We recently had an entire service led by the local Deaf Chaplaincy Team, complete with the reading of wedding banns in British Sign Language. It is important to see people whom society labels as 'disabled' as those who have gifts to offer and not just as those who need to be on the receiving end.

Do not make assumptions. For instance, just because two people are both 'legally blind' it does not mean that they have the same level of functional sight. Do not look at difficulties—look at possibilities, at what that person could bring. I was at college with someone who had been affected by Thalidomide. There were some things he could not do but not many. I have a godson who is completely blind. When he was younger he rode his tricycle round the house, at some speed, without hitting any of the furniture.

Ask the person themselves what they can do and what they would like to do. You might be surprised. To involve someone with a specific disability may be as simple as doing a task in a different way. I have heard a blind person 'read' the Bible in church (by recording the reading beforehand and having it played back through earphones as he then spoke the words out). A person with cerebral palsy is able to have a ministry as a public speaker by having a headset with a microphone rather than a microphone on a stand. Modern technology is a real boon here. A wide variety of aids, software programs and hardware are readily available. You may not be aware of them but the person with the disability is likely to be. Talk to them and work out the practicalities together. There may be costs involved, so take that into account in your budgeting. You may find help available from various grant sources, beginning with your Local Authority, who will certainly have advisors if not access to funds themselves. People's attitudes can be more significant barriers than the practical.

Virtual volunteering is an area in which people with certain disabilities may have a lot to offer, even those you might not immediately think of, such as visual impairment (there is a lot of software around to help them to read text). To involve all parts of the Body means involving volunteers of all abilities in all sorts of ways.

Do not be afraid to recruit people with a mental illness or disability. You may not even be aware that you are likely to have congregation members in this category. As I wrote this, I stopped to think and five excellent volunteers immediately came to mind, two with schizophrenia, one with bi-polar disorder and two with special educational needs—each with much to contribute, each valued members of their churches. People on the autistic spectrum may well have great artistic talents or significant skills with IT. Both 'real' and 'virtual' volunteering may offer a real chance for many people with a wide range of mental health issues to contribute a great deal and to be significantly built up themselves.[28]

If the disability comes on with old age, what can be done to make it easier for individuals to continue serving? Does someone doing a reading or leading prayers have to stand or to walk to the reading desk? If someone can still clean the church brass but can no longer get to church, could another member of the church take the brass to them—and have a good chat and cup of tea while they share the task?

Above all, let us not continue to reinforce the image of those with a disability people as passive beneficiaries of other's volunteering. Rather, we should regard them and promote them as individuals who have a considerable contribution to make. To involve as wide a range as possible of members of the Body of Christ is not only good for them—it is good for the whole Body of the Church and its witness.[29]

Involving all ages

What might you do to involve younger members of your church more? A big influence on my life was through becoming involved with a series of roles at church when I was younger. Being encouraged and taken seriously has been part of the path that has led to the job I am doing now. I was a sidesperson at the age of twelve, reading, doing drama and prayers at 13, preaching occasionally at 16. I was on our church council at 16. We had a youth group committee that planned our own programme, and we ran much of it ourselves.

In our church we encourage children to come on to our reading rota as soon as they feel confident enough, and take part in all-age services in a whole variety of ways. We had a junior church council (ages seven to 16) that met before our official one, made comments on relevant items, and raised their own points, and we have just started a youth band to lead music in our family services, with children as young as seven.

Children can be choir members or servers or take the collection. At one church, children rang the bell. They loved that. What else might children do? I have seen them arrange recycling schemes, run Fairtrade stalls, do litter-picking around the community (we did this as part of our holiday club). There are all sorts of spin-offs for the children themselves and within the congregation and wider community, as people of different ages help one another and build relationships.

There are some issues to bear in mind. One is that involving teenagers and younger children will not necessarily save you time. They are likely to need a higher level of guidance and supervision than older volunteers, and are less likely to be able to take the initiative while an event is taking place. This will mean someone keeping a close eye on them. Recently we involved some teenagers in a project for older people. There were lots of positives about this, but there were times when they were standing around as a group, not quite sure what to do next. We needed to plan their involvement a little more carefully.[30]

Another issue is that listening to ideas of young people is good, but you may need to do more than just support them in what they come up with. When we asked a school to involve a group from their community service project in running a stall for a local gala, they came up with a variety of ideas with great enthusiasm and carried their chosen activity out with energy. Sadly, the idea they had settled on was not so attractive to the younger and older people there, nor did they have the confidence to 'sell' what they were doing around the event. They left early, rather disconsolate, and the organisers later had to de-brief them to try and boost their confidence, which had taken quite a knock. As can be the danger with any group, their own likes and interests had steered their ideas rather too strongly. Simpler ideas, which had been proposed and would have been easier to implement, had not been adequately championed.

Getting the balance right of allowing young people to 'own' the project fully while offering the wisdom that comes from experience is not easy. As we will discuss later, allowing people to make mistakes is OK and can be an excellent learning opportunity, but this should be an incidental rather than a deliberate aim. As adults we need to do all we can, and in a way that respects younger people's input, to help them succeed and flourish. If we do not, the danger is that they may not be prepared to volunteer again, and you may have lost some great talent for a future life of volunteering.

Volunteering as a family

We do not have to involve children with certain activities and their parents with others. With all the pressures on time today, and considering that different members of the family can be at many different events during a week, how about promoting volunteering as a way of spending time together as a family? The bell-ringing churchwarden I mentioned earlier has a daughter who has followed him into the tower, as has his wife. During school holidays the lady who cuts the lawn in front of our parish centre is accompanied by her daughter. When I used to act as a volunteer chaplain abroad, the whole family got involved in the game of 'spot the British cars and put a leaflet under the windscreen wipers'. I have known whole families who have offered themselves for gardening duty through a charity auction and others who work together at Christian summer camps.

Could there be opportunities you could develop that would allow families to spend constructive time together, and benefit the church and community? All the activities listed in the previous section would be possibilities, but here are a few more. How about getting a family to organise the collection of food for the local food bank or night shelter, or books and toys for a local refugee project? Each year our church runs 'Angel Tree', a project to send presents on behalf of women in prison to their children. Children, alongside their parents, help to choose and wrap the presents. Our children have helped me deliver Christian Aid envelopes (and older children could perhaps help collect, provided you were not too far away). Others have helped deliver our church calendar. Is there something focused in your own church (family cleaning team, anyone?). A whole family had joined our church's 'welcomers' team. Others help with the coffee after the service.

How about fundraising: running a coffee morning at home, making jam or greetings cards together, growing seedlings to sell for one of your supported missions? There could be lobbying for a cause, either remotely or joining in national rallies as a family. Community gardening for the green-fingered? An inter-generational computer club? Perhaps a local residential home would value visitors—and those visitors could be helping with crafts, reading to the visually impaired or playing games, not just engaging in conversation. Musical families could run a concert. Or how about inviting older church members for Sunday tea, with the children doing the bulk of the hosting and entertaining? Or helping to decorate someone's home? Be creative with your thinking. All this will teach the children that being a Christian is not just about coming to church—it is about fulfilling the challenge of Matthew 25:31–46.

If we are to encourage family volunteering, we need to work at making it family-*friendly* volunteering. We have to recognise that volunteers have other responsibilities such as caring for children, partners, parents and running a household (a good principle to keep in mind for all volunteers). You might need to time-shift some activities. You could offer baby-sitting or perhaps in this context what some call 'granny-sitting'. And of course 'granny' might well be interested in volunteering herself. Three- or even four-generational families volunteering together is a great picture.

For some people at least, volunteering is learned by being part of a family tradition. My wife, who has a Salvation Army background, remembers going round the hospital wards with the band on Christmas morning. Only after doing this did they return home to open presents. If you as a parent feel volunteering is important then, as in other important areas of life, involve the children. Developing habits early is important in volunteering as in many other areas of life.[31]

Volunteering as a home group

In churches that follow a cell church model, it is expected that each cell will take on some practical or mission-focused activity that they do together. This is something that any church's home or house groups could be encouraged to do.

This has benefits such as:

- being a cause that is very close to the members, as it is decided upon by the group itself
- involving a group of people working together who know each other well, regularly pray for each other and already have good relationships of trust and mutual support
- being something small scale, with easily visible benefits

Home groups are a good place to think about the place of service as part of Christian commitment, allied with some central teaching.[32]

New monasticism

Some people's commitment to their faith goes a whole level deeper. In 'new monasticism' people commit themselves to a 'rule of life' based on those followed by established monastic communities, usually while remaining in 'normal' jobs. At least some such rules of life involve being committed to activities for the benefit of those living locally—'being community and making a difference to the community we live in', 'a focus on the way we live in but not of contemporary culture', 'inspiring people to follow God', 'learning to be activist and contemplative,' 'more available for God and more present to the world'.[33] Some such movements actually have shared community houses, although not many do in the UK as yet.

By becoming part of such a community, people commit themselves to God and to each other in a wholehearted way. They have a passion for the mission of the church and the difference faith can make. Voluntary community work thus becomes a part of the rule of life such groups follow, helping them have stability and purpose. This approach is growing in popularity among Generations X and Y as it fits with their wholehearted approach to whatever they are committed.

Chapter 5

Recruiting your volunteers

I was running a communication training event. As I went round the group at the start, asking where people were from and why they were there, one person had only a single reason, 'Because the vicar asked me!' She proved to be an enthusiastic group member and went on to make a significant difference to her parish's magazine and media coverage.

'We need someone to...'

We do need to ask people to volunteer. It sounds obvious, but sometimes we just put up a notice and hope. Not everyone looks at the notice board or reads the notice sheet. Perhaps you do not get a response because what is clear in your mind is not so clear in the notice. It may not sound that interesting or you may not have included enough detail for people to grasp what it is really about. On the other hand, perhaps the task sounds just too scary in a few words of black and white.

Many experts on volunteering suggest that this is the worst way to recruit. Yet if it *never* worked, surely we would have stopped doing it by now? I have had a number of very successful volunteers come forward that way. So, if you are going to give out a general request, are some ways to do this better than others? Tim Morgan of Granger Community Church, Indiana, US has four rules about them:

- **Less is better than more.** In other words, use this method sparingly. The more you do it, the less effective it will be.
- **New is better than old.** Use appeals from the front for new work. People love to get in on the 'ground floor' of something.
- **Vacant is better than forced.** Do not make people feel guilty. Rather appeal to their gifts and vision. It is better to leave a vacancy unfilled, even an important one, than to have the wrong person in it.
- **Outcomes are better than inputs.** Talk more about the results of the ministry, what might be achieved, rather than the work required.[34]

If you make a general appeal for volunteers, you might get the 'wrong' person. That is a risk you take. You may need to bring to bear your best diplomatic skills in such an instance. If you have a proper system of selection/probation (see Chapter 9), it should not be so much of a problem, as the offer is not the end of the process. And, sometimes, by a general appeal you will get a great volunteer whom you might otherwise not have discovered. This happened to me recently. I had asked one or two likely candidates for a job but to no avail. I made a request, and the following week someone offered who had both the time and the skills to do it.

I tend to use a both/and strategy here. Do the general notice *and* target people specifically. There may be some whom you would never think of asking (as in the example above) who will respond to a notice. You may not know enough about people's skills or past experience to ask the right potential candidate. Alternatively, there are those who would never put themselves forward but are happy to be asked. Some people need to be drawn out. This book is itself the fruit of my being asked to tackle the subject!

So ask

Some people may just be waiting to be asked. When a lady in my church retired, I did not want to pounce on her immediately. (A six months 'sabbatical' after finishing work is a very good idea. I would suggest it is official church policy.) In responding, she told me she was 'climbing up the walls' with very little to do. Not only did she respond to my initial request, but she also made several other suggestions as to how she might help, one of which led to a very significant role in the wider community that we had been struggling to fill for some months. I felt gently rebuked that I had not thought more about using her many gifts.

That kind of unexpected response reminds me of another bit of experience in recruiting: do not always ask the same people, the 'usual suspects'. Of course you should ask individuals who you think might be interested—it would be foolish not to—but I encourage you to think more widely. Once we were struggling to find a female leader for one of our youth groups. All the younger women I could think of were fully committed or not available. Then I remembered that one of our older members had once told me she had helped with youth work in her younger days, and although that had been many years earlier, I thought it worth asking her again. She was delighted and was a faithful member of the team for some time after that. There is great value in knowing your church members well enough to be able to link them with opportunities when they arise.

Perhaps we do not ask because of that polite British sentiment of not wanting to put anyone 'on the spot'? Perhaps it is that we had drilled into us as children that 'those who ask, don't get'. If you do not ask, then people will not know, and you will not get either! Be careful of being too 'pushy', however. Make it clear what you are asking them to do. Paint a picture of how you feel they might contribute, then give them space to think and pray before they have to respond.

Face to face is usually the best way to ask someone but sometimes an email, spelling things out, perhaps even including a 'role description' and asking them to 'think and pray about it and we'll have a chat next week', might be a good way of preparing the ground. An email can help to prepare the person and can set the scene for a more constructive conversation. Always, always ask in such a way that the person asked feels they can say 'no'. People can find it easier to say 'no' to an email, with less embarrassment. If you give them time to think about it with no pressure, they may, however, respond 'yes' when their immediate response to a direct request might have been 'no'.

When you do ask, have all the details you need to hand. Just to say, 'We need someone to help with the children's work,' is not all that helpful. Are you asking them to tell stories, lead worship, help with the craftwork, or prepare the squash and biscuits? Yes, I know, some people do all of these, but they are quite discrete sets of gifts. So, whatever you need, ask for it specifically. Do not expect all your volunteers to do everything. Breaking down the task to 'bite-size chunks' can make the task seem more manageable and, through being clearer, make requests more likely to receive a positive response.

'It's the minister'

Be careful, too, how often you ask, or people may come to dread meeting you. As a teenager, I would be enjoying a Saturday evening when, every few weeks, always around 8pm, there would be a phone call from the vicar asking me to do the prayers in the service the following day. This was not the best strategy. One thing I do is to keep notes of who has done what and when. And if, when I ask, people say, 'I can't just now, but maybe next time,' I make a note of that too and next time I start with them. Ask people occasionally, and then devise a rota which goes out weeks or even months in advance. You may need to ask only once to achieve a regular involvement.

It does not always have to be the minister who asks, although it often is. Those who are already enjoying volunteering will be your best recruiters, your 'ambassadors' or 'champions'. Make the most of them. The next time you want a notice given out relating to their group, ask them to do it, rather than giving the notice yourself.

This is very much my approach to finding new churchwardens (elders with legal responsibilities). I ask my current wardens who they think might be suitable and also ask them to make the first approach. One year the retiring wardens wrote an article for our magazine about what their role involved, how they felt about it, how they saw it as their calling. This approach has consistently brought in some really excellent people, including individuals I may never have thought of asking. It also means the church is less likely to end up with churchwardens who are 'clones' of me.

Volunteers recruiting their friends can be very effective too. Ask your existing volunteers to keep the recruitment of new helpers at the forefront of their mind at all times, not just when there is a specific need. After all, how many groups could not do with one or two extra people to help out?

Having too many volunteers may be a luxury you would love to have. If it does happen, be careful. It is not good to have helpers who feel they are wasting their time. One church had too many people turn up to help unload food from a lorry. The leader decided to park the lorry further away in order to make the line of people longer! I was appalled. It would not have taken much thought for some of those in the line to be very cross indeed. If you find you have too many people for a current need, think hard about what else you could do, for example, whether you could expand by creating a parallel group. While on placement at a church during ministerial training, a small group of us offered to start a home-based study group. The vicar said we should start two groups, so we could train up twice as many people.

Another advantage of having more volunteers than you need for a regular event is to be able to run a rota, so that not every volunteer is on duty every time. A growing number of people find it difficult, if not impossible, to commit to a weekly activity. Developing a team in this way also means that a wider number of members can get a deeper experience of the activity concerned, which should help in the ongoing support of the project. A proper rota is also a good way to prevent volunteers getting over-tired and over-stretched.

Preparing the ground

How much does the responsibility of offering our gifts for God's service figure in your preaching programme? How often do you talk about the joy of serving and on the biblical image of the Body of Christ? And what about in your house group studies?

You might have presentations on particular aspects of your church's work as a regular feature of your services, with a prayer focus. Use these opportunities for appealing for extra help if you need it. Use brief interviews in services and at other occasions. It does not have to be a major event with a lot of planning. You might simply ask someone, 'What would you like us to pray for this week, for the children's club/Street Angels/community café?'

You could develop a whole service around the idea of volunteering, or even a series of services. Lent would be a good time to do this, exploring different angles of what discipleship means. You could run a series at other times of the year, as we have, on the different spiritual gifts.[35] Exploring this in small groups as well as in worship would give a good opportunity for people to reflect on what gifts God has given them. The idea of using our skills for God should be a regular part of your teaching, in the same way that most churches would include regular sermons on financial giving.

Another way you might like to try would be having a skills/gift audit—asking what gifts people have, and if they would be prepared to use them in some way or other.[36] This can be very helpful and assist the church in discovering gifts within the congregation of which you were previously unaware. However comprehensive you make the list, you should leave space for people to add those skills you have not thought of.

If you do this exercise, make sure you follow up all the offers in good time, even those you think you may not be able to use immediately as if you don't, you are actually likely to discourage people. A colleague was wondering why no one had volunteered for the project she was organising. There had in fact been an offer but it had not been followed up, and the one who had offered ended up feeling rejected, unhappy, slighted. Such a person is far less likely to volunteer again.

In order to do this I suggest bringing together a small group to plan and carry it out. Larger churches might even develop a dedicated group to work on volunteering. However you decide to include this in your church's programme, it is important that there is active encouraging of people, not just a passive waiting for them to respond.

And also

General notices, calls within sermons and presentations, individual conversations. What other ways could you try? If you are a larger church, how about holding a 'job fair'? Have a series of stalls, with each group 'selling' their particular project as really exciting and worthwhile.

Some years ago my church held a harvest service with a difference: a 'harvest of gifts'. This was more to do with offering to God what each person did during the week, but it could easily be adapted to include, or even focus on, what members do as a volunteer. It could also be very informative as you learn what people do outside the church as well as within your own programmes.

Another way would be to develop your church's annual meeting. Rather than having just verbal reports, you could use displays showing what that particular group does—photographs, stories and perhaps some hands-on demonstrations (bearing in mind the maxim 'I hear, I forget; I see, I remember; I do, I understand'). This has the potential not only to make that meeting more interesting, but also to let the wider church know just how much goes on (activities that take place during the week can often be a mystery to those not involved).

Keep 'banging the drum' about how interesting/valuable/needed people are. Regularly run articles about volunteers in any magazine or newsletter you may have, getting a current volunteer to write it. People are interested in people, so those articles will prove popular in any case and they will encourage those already involved. Regular inclusion of such articles will give the message: 'lots of people in this church volunteer. I wonder if I should?'

A larger church may want to appoint a volunteer coordinator. Volunteers with particular roles should certainly take on the main effort for recruiting into their teams. In our church, for example, it is the children's work coordinator who keeps an eye out for potential new recruits for children's groups, and the bereavement coordinator who looks for those with suitable gifting to visit. As our church is not particularly large, I am usually kept in the loop, but they know they can act and 'sign people up' without referring every decision back to me.

Busy people

I will make a confession at this point. I know it is important to ask, and yet I am often rather reluctant to do so. I do not want to exhaust people or make them feel that they must use all their spare time on church programmes. Everyone needs time for themselves and their families, but also the opportunity to be witnesses in their other roles in life. I want them to be involved in local community groups, with other local and national charities, with a whole range of organisations. I believe this is the wider mission of God for which we are called to work, and I will return to this topic in the final chapter.

Common wisdom has it that those who are already committed are often the best people to ask for a new role. Indeed one of my friends who is heavily involved in volunteering actually has an email address of 'ask.a.busy.person@...'! I try not to ask those who I know are already highly committed to take on something else, although it is often difficult to stop them doing more. For those at the other end of the spectrum, it may just be that committing to a particular voluntary activity actually improves their commitment to other aspects, including worship. I can think of a number of people who attend church only when they are on a rota for a role.

Getting that toe in the water...

Bill Hybels talks about how at Willow Creek Community Church in Illinois, they have a system called 'first serve',[37] a kind of 'try before you buy' system. They encourage people to come along to an event once, and then assess it. This sounds a reasonable idea. It might just encourage someone with its 'no commitment' approach, but I am not sure whether just attending once would give you a real idea of an activity. I would suggest allowing someone to come along and try something for a few weeks, even if you did not have a formal scheme as such. I would still have a 'probationary period' of three or six months (see Chapter 9) after they have decided to commit, both for their benefit and for yours as an organisation. If you both feel there is a real 'fit', then longer-term value will be assured.

What happens if, after a few weeks or longer, your new volunteer finds that what they are trying does not work for them? They have not changed their mind about helping, but they do not feel suited for that particular role. Just because someone offers, or has even been asked to do something, does not mean their commitment is fixed at that point. They may offer to help with the crèche while they are in fact better equipped to visit the housebound, or they discover (after psyching themselves up for it in the first place) that public reading or prayer is not their thing but small groups are. Making it easier for people to step in and, after reflection, out if necessary, giving them every chance to change their mind, will also be a great recruiting tool.

As well as actually trying something out, another option is to allow prospective helpers simply to observe. This is perhaps an especially useful approach with the more 'techy' roles, such as working a sound desk or a computer and projector, as there may be a real 'fear factor' to overcome or a feeling that 'I couldn't possibly do that'.

Starting small and working up is a good way in. There are many stories of someone very successful in their career who started right at the bottom and worked up. This is true of a friend of mine who ended up very senior in the management of a major supermarket chain, having begun working as the 'egg boy', checking each box for broken eggs. Equally, I know people who have started off helping out at an annual event and have gone on to run the event in due course (indeed in two cases made a career out of running such events on a national level).

... or dive in head first

Bill Hybels talks about encouraging people to 'just jump in',[38] experiment to find what they are good at and enjoy and to keep trying until they find their passion. Sometimes volunteering for something that is *not* in your immediate comfort zone is good too. Here is a personal story to illustrate this.

When I lived in Guildford, someone came to our church to ask for volunteers for an evening café for homeless people (yes, even in Guildford). I felt strongly compelled to offer to help, in spite of such work being way outside my comfort zone. I had little previous experience and I am not a particularly extravert character. To be honest, I am not very good with dirt and smells either. I hoped that the organisers would recognise my lack of natural gifting for the work. Sadly, they received my offer with enthusiasm. So there I would be once a month on a Sunday evening, making sandwiches, serving drinks and washing up, and in between chatting to some of those who came. Every evening when we finished I felt a huge relief, yet the experience of that couple of years has stayed with me. I can still easily recall the faces and stories of some of the people there. I do not have any amazing stories of lives turned round. I cannot say that I am a hugely better person for the experience, or that I now regularly help with an equivalent local group. I was, though, encouraged and built up through doing it. I hope I played a part in encouraging others too, both those who came for a meal and a shower and some of the other volunteers. Whatever else I did or did not do, I was sharing a very small amount of the salt and light that we are called to be as Christians. I was being the part of the Body that helped others. And if I had not been there, the Body would have been lessened or other parts would have had to work harder.

Sometimes it is worth encouraging people to do something that doesn't seem a 100 per cent natural fit, with appropriate support and training, because they might find they *are* good at something they would never have otherwise tried to do. I have known a number of people who have said to me 'Oh, I could never do that,' only to find that they can.

Attracting the new generations

Following on from my comments on Gen Y in an earlier chapter, when thinking of recruiting younger people, you will especially need to bear in mind such things as the following:

- Help them realise that they have something valuable to offer. This can be a real issue. They may think volunteering is 'for older people' unless they have personal experience of it in the family.
- Building up their self-confidence. They may not realise that they have skills.
- Offering time slots and patterns of commitment that suit their life style, which may include part-time work on irregular rotas.
- Offer them a chance to volunteer with friends. You may need to take a group as a whole or you will not get any of them, even if some 'fit' your needs better than others.
- Go with the grain. Find out what their enthusiasms are, and see if there are opportunities that match these. If some have a low boredom threshold, try to avoid breaching it.

These issues are not the case for all young people. I can think of some for whom none of the above points would apply, but equally I can think of many who would tick most, if not all, of these metaphorical boxes.

Traditionally, Sunday schools have often recruited children who have been through the classes to come back and help once they are older. This can be the start of lifelong responsibility. One of the older ladies in my congregation started her volunteering in just such a role, along with singing in the choir. Later she led the Mothers' Union, became churchwarden and acted as verger. Now in her 80s, she is still a keyholder of the church and helps with coffee mornings.

Our annual holiday club has a number of teenage helpers each year. Some of them are recruited when the families continue to bring younger children and the older siblings miss coming along, so we offer them an opportunity. Others join us in their teens. Younger people helping in this way must be given a real role rather than just being there to 'make up numbers' or to continue coming along by the 'back door' as it were. In our case, involvement in drama, crafts and music are these main roles as well as helping in smaller groups, especially with the younger children.

As with the older generations, young volunteers are your best ambassadors and often better recruiters than church leaders, so work with those young people who are closest to the church, most confident or who have been drawn in already through their parents to recruit others.

The CV effect

How much note should we take of 'the CV effect'? These days this might be very important for a younger volunteer (and perhaps for a not-so-young, too). Students these days are conscious of the need to build up evidence for their 'personal statements' in future university/higher education or job applications. Those in higher education are, by all accounts, more likely to volunteer than the general cohort of young people, but they may also well expect a more stimulating experience. They will certainly expect a higher standard of organisation, and will want to contribute more to the planning as well as the execution. Indeed, it would be foolish not to make the most of what they can bring.

You may find you have to 'sell' your opportunities harder, even within your congregation and certainly if you are setting out to recruit people more widely. Will you be able to offer some sort of formal recognition or training? Will the volunteers gain new skills? Might they become valued in the local community or a part of new networks? Are they likely to be somewhere they might make new friends? Will volunteering give them more insights or understanding that will help them in their work or personal relationships? Could it give them skills, for example in leading a team, that will benefit them in their work? Will they gain self-esteem, not just recognition? This area might seem a bit sensitive for a Christian—should people not do a job simply because it is a worthwhile thing to do? Yes, but there is also the principle that 'the worker deserves his wages' (1 Timothy 5:18). Building people up as individuals is to the benefit of the wider Body as well.

Saying 'yes' helps

A lot of this chapter has been about going out and trying to find volunteers. What about when volunteers come to you? They may well offer something you cannot use immediately. Be nonetheless encouraging. Thank them and work with them to see if there are any existing areas where they may be able to use their particular gifts and talents or, if not, see if you can find something new in which they could be used. Perhaps the new volunteers will start a whole new area of work.

There is always fundraising! A lady in our congregation is a talented and prodigious knitter and she offered her skill. Where could we use such a talent? Then we thought about our building project, for which she now regularly takes commissions. She gets the costs covered for a hobby she enjoys anyway, and she also gets the satisfaction of contributing to a wider need. People get a bespoke item of clothing and the church gets more money in its funds. A real win–win situation.

In fact, knitting can be an excellent way of bringing people together for a good social time and a good cause. How many squares of blanket knitted in UK churches are in refugee camps around the world, I wonder, and how many 'Trauma Teddies' (knitted teddy bears that are given to children in crisis situations—see, for example, www.teddiesfortragedies.org.uk)? Perhaps that project could take place in a local residential home, led by church volunteers?

... looking wider afield

Going back to one of the points with which I began this chapter, occasionally you may have to leave an important post vacant for a short while. You should not simply be passive about it, however, and accept the situation long-term. If you do know of anyone yourself, how about approaching other local churches to see if they have someone who could help? A radical idea, I know, but since when has the Body of Christ finished at your own church's door or address list?

If you are struggling to find a volunteer from your own church, why not see if there are people in the wider community who would help? You could ask your local newspaper if they would run a feature. This is generally quite easy, but you will need to make it a story for them by linking it to a special event (which you can, of course, create especially) or anniversary, or make it a 'human interest' piece. A photo opportunity of the group in action will make it more attractive too. Many Local Authorities will have a department to support and encourage volunteering and so do adult education centres. Some churches have had considerable success in this.[39]

This is a classic situation in which you need to be aware of the generational differences and their preferred sources of information. One case has stuck in my mind that, while not directly relevant to recruitment, is a good example of what I mean. A group of local churches were running a treasure hunt-style quiz and had signed up a local radio station to put out the clues. Halfway through the week they had not had any response. The reason was that they had put the clues out on the local BBC radio station (which they, from the Boomers and Silent Generation, listened to) rather than the commercial radio station that the younger generations used. The same applies for recruiting. Talk to the relevant generation and find out what works for them.

If the opportunity would suit a young person, you could contact a local school, college or university chaplaincy or Christian Union. Young people might be looking for opportunities for community service, for example for the Duke of Edinburgh scheme, or going through the Scout and Guide awards. Perhaps your church could provide what is needed. Universities often need placements for students in a wide range of subjects, while a lot of secondary schools have their own schemes for encouraging community involvement. Some of these are specifically aimed at those less academically capable or otherwise in need of extra support. These helpers may not have the initiative others have and may exhibit challenging behaviour, but there is a special joy from seeing such young people realise that they have something to give, that others are relying on them and wanting them around to help.

Some of the larger companies, and some smaller ones too, encourage staff to spend a number of hours volunteering.[40] You could also try contacting your local Rotary or Lions group.

As well as sending 'adverts' to such general groups, how about targeting specific groups for specific needs? If you're looking for help with the church grounds, you could ask the local gardening club or place an advert at the garden centre. For banners, how about the embroidery guild? For help with documenting building and contents, or backgrounds for data projections slides, you could try the local photographic society (it worked for us).

And why not use one of the volunteering websites to advertise?[41] Nothing ventured...

Outside the congregation of faith?

Unless you have a very strict policy of accepting only Christians for your work (and if you do, then the above section is not a route I recommend you go down), then you are likely to have people on your team who do not have your faith. Involving others who do not share such a commitment is not without its challenges, but the best practice encouraged in this book will work equally well with those of any faith or none. In one of our churches' parents and toddler group the leadership is shared between a church member and a number of the non-church parents. They respect the Christian ethos of the group, which is clear but low key.

Involving those outside your immediate community can have all sorts of benefits, like making the church seem more integrated with the wider community, exposing people to what Christians are really like, and so many more. When I was myself a volunteer at a youth and community project in Liverpool, we regularly encouraged young people who had been through the club to remain with us and volunteer themselves. The challenges here included a wide range of behaviour issues, inappropriate language and more. When I returned to the project some 20 years later, one of those young people was still a volunteer and a member of the wider church community. Another, who had later been employed on the project, had become both a member of the church and a respected local politician. They were also some of the few young people I had known there who were not either unemployed or in jail. I know just how much time and effort had been invested in these people, and some of the heartache this policy had led to over the years, but the benefits to the individuals, and the project, were considerable.

Chapter 6

Teams, training, trust—and taking risks

Being part of a team is important in many ways, not least for the motivation of your volunteers. A good team will be very supportive of its members. People who know one another well, who care for one another at a deep level and who regularly pray for each other are often the best to offer that 'frontline' support to each other. A good team will be creative, dynamic and effective. A good team will do what it has been set up to do.

There are four classic stages of team development:[42]

1. **Forming:** coming together, getting to know one another.
2. **Storming:** settling down, finding what works and what does not. Things can be a bit 'choppy' as the name suggests.
3. **Norming:** working out the rules, getting into your stride.
4. **Performing:** knowing each other well enough to work together well and usually developing a real care and concern for one another.

There is plenty of material available that explores these stages in detail, so I do not propose to say more here. I would like to say a little about a fifth stage that is often forgotten: adjourning. The adjourning stage happens when the group has achieved its original purpose or when the time allotted for the group activity has run out. This is the stage at which most churches are very poor.

Do you have groups that have long ago finished their original task? ('We used to be the young wives,' and no one is under 60, for example.) When I ran management meetings at CMS, I regularly had an item on the Agenda called 'abandonment'—what should we stop doing? Occasionally we would find something that had run its day and start the process of closing it down. I have tried it with some of our church council agendas. The problem is that people usually think I am joking or that this is just a pious wish. I must try harder! I believe this is a question you should regularly ask of every group you have. Stopping a group that has passed its 'best before' date will free up volunteers to work on other tasks you have wanted to do but for which you have not been able to find the people or resources—until now.

Understanding one another in teams

A crucial part of working with teams is getting on with each other. Are there those with whom you really struggle, who somehow rub you up the wrong way? You cannot get 'into their skin' and understand how their mind works. There are a number of tools available that will increase both your self-understanding and your understanding of others. The best known are the Myers-Briggs (MBTI)[43] and the Enneagram[44] Personality Type Indicators. I have used both and find the former the more helpful.

Also, in a team of any size, you will find some people who love to get events going but lose interest after the start-up, those who come up with loads of ideas (some not always practical), and others who seem just good all-round 'team players'. As with personality types, there are various schemes that can help you explore these roles further. The one I know best is the Belbin Team Roles.[45] Although developed for the workplace, it can be equally useful in helping volunteer teams. Other systems include the Margerison-McCann Team Management System,[46] or the Gallup-created 'StrengthsFinder'.[47]

If you are in a group of any size, you may well find exploring one or more of these as a team very valuable. Even if you do not use any of these formal tools, it is really helpful gaining an idea of people's preferences, strengths and weaknesses ('allowable' weaknesses in MBTI terminology). It makes sense as it will help you to ask people to do the things they will both be good at and enjoy the most. It is best to have team members play to their strengths, and this will help team harmony.

A growing team

One issue the standard model of team formation does not take adequately into account is that surrounding the addition of new people into a well established team. The team members know each other well; they have their ways of working. If you are the team leader, think carefully about how the new member will be inducted into the team and introduced to their role. In the first few weeks check whether others are giving them enough work to do. Keep an eye on them when it comes to the coffee break. Is anyone talking to them? Teams may not deliberately sideline the new person, but it may be happening all the same. Try to imagine how you felt when you started something new. It is always good to ask a new volunteer how they are getting on, but remember that as you need to help the new person, so you might need to help the team as well.

Team leadership

Each team will have a leader, but that leader should not make every single decision. As team leader you do not need to be the source of wisdom on all topics. If you have discovered people's strengths and preferences, then these should come into play in the decision-making process. If a team member knows a lot more than anyone else on a subject, it makes sense that they take the lead in their area of expertise.

As I wrote that last paragraph, a small warning light flashed in my head. There are leaders, more than there should be, who seem only to pick new team members who are like them. And there are others who are not comfortable with people in their team knowing more than they do about the job in hand. If a leader has both those characteristics, it can be disastrous. 'I don't employ people to disagree with me,' said one senior leader, so few new ideas ever got through in that team. If a leader, professional or volunteer, feels like that, it will severely limit the team's output and effectiveness.

In volunteer teams people are very likely to have skills and experience from their professional lives that they can bring to bear, if they are allowed. A lot of my ministry has involved being a visiting preacher or 'consultant' to churches. In one church vestry I was introduced to someone as 'my head server' (someone who helps out during communion). What I was not told until later by another member of that church was that this person also happened to be a very senior executive with a major oil corporation. To the vicar he was simply 'my head server'. He was never asked his professional advice on church issues, because that was 'the vicar's domain'. To me that is both a dreadful waste of good talent and a poor way to treat someone.

Let even the newest volunteer, whatever their experience, offer ideas and suggestions for improvement. In fact, a new volunteer might be the very best person to do this as they see with fresh eyes. They are not caught up in the 'well, that's the way we've always done it' attitude that can grow in even the best teams. Do not stop asking for input from all team members. I am not a great lover of 'feedback' forms after each and every event, although it is helpful to know that you are on the right lines. But a good team debrief after each session can be helpful (and keep it brief, no more than, say, five minutes at the end of an evening's activity). You can have more in-depth meetings at the end of each 'term', reflecting back on how things have gone in order to help you plan and prepare for the next sessions. For a major event, trying to do a debrief immediately afterwards is not going to work. People will be tired and, if things have not gone as well as you had hoped, disappointed. Build in to your planning schedule a meeting a few weeks afterwards and make it a celebration party too.

If a volunteer comes up with a good idea, then make sure it is acted upon. Praising someone for a good idea will have a limited effect if it never sees the light of day, and if that happens too often people will stop offering ideas. If the idea is for a new development then, why not put the onus back on to the one who has offered it? Rather than saying, 'Great, I'll get this on our next agenda and find some people to get involved,' say, 'Great, how can I help you develop that idea?' As it is their idea, they are likely to have the passion and commitment to drive it forward. It will not become just another thing on the growing 'to do' list of the team leader. This is a great way to grow not just new leaders but new teams. The leader's job is to offer all the support they can.

The right skills

You do not simply build a team out of those willing to take part. To create an effective team you need people with the appropriate skills. However much someone loves a task, however much time they give to it, however enthusiastic they are, if they do not have the right skills, they will not do a good job. This is true across all fields but I will use an example with which I am very familiar— church magazines.

Over the years I have led design workshops and run competitions to discover the best of design skills. Like many areas of expertise, it is easy to underestimate the skills and time you need to do a good job. With so much computer use today, many people think they know about graphic design. The average church wouldn't be expected to use high-end Desk Top Publishing software, but if your magazine still looks as if is produced on a typewriter and stencil-cut Roneo (and I saw one like that just the other day) then you, or your volunteers, need to do something about it.

I hope you can do the 'translation' of this example into other areas: the children's worker who 'knows just what to do', because they have had children of their own; the cook who thinks they can prepare meals for 50 people because they regularly produce meals for four. It is not a matter of whether something is done by a volunteer or a professional that makes the difference. It is about being done by a volunteer (or professional for that matter) with the right skills, equipment or training. Equipment and training can be provided.

Training

Few volunteers come forward with all the skills they need. Even if they do, they will need further training in due course. Lifelong learning is important to prevent us from getting stale, to stimulate new ideas, and to keep up with the changing ideas of what makes for best practice. Training means investing in people, showing you value them and helping them to become even more effective. Build it in to your church budget; keep up to date with what is on offer; learn best practice from other volunteers. Each person should have the opportunity to develop.

By all means organise training yourself, but do not reinvent the wheel. See what you can do with other churches locally, sharing resources and costs. Most larger church organisations will have specialists who will happily, indeed enthusiastically, organise training events in their area of expertise. Also, many such organisations have excellent facilities and regularly offer courses.

Build people's involvement up slowly. The last thing you want to do is drop anyone in at the deep end. Leading the worship for the old people's service on your second occasion or taking charge of the youth group after a month is a sure way to lose a volunteer and to frighten off others as they get to hear about what happened. And believe me, they will. Just as satisfied volunteers are your best ambassadors, dissatisfied or disappointed people will have a strong negative effect.

Taking risks

It is important to take risks with volunteers. Micromanaging works no better with them than with paid staff. Making every decision yourself, keeping a tight rein on what is done, coming up with all the major ideas, and dotting every 'i' and crossing every 't' might make you comfortable and it might even mean a group runs perfectly well, but it will not develop your volunteers and certainly will not encourage others to develop their own gifts of leadership. You should allow, even encourage, people to take risks. If that scares you, bear with me and I'll explain.

One of my father's sayings was 'The man who never took a risk never did anything'. I guess that must have lodged deep within my character, as it is a central part of my approach to leadership. I am a permission-giving leader, which means that I take risks. I am inclined to trust someone until they prove otherwise. If anyone comes to me with an idea I am most likely to say, 'Go ahead'. I say 'inclined' and 'most likely' because another leadership role is to judge the severity of a risk. This is more than simply the likelihood of a person succeeding or failing, because failure is not inevitably a disaster. It is rather an issue of how serious a 'disaster' it might be.

On a leadership course I attended we were introduced to the concept of picturing an organisation as a ship, and mistakes or failures as occurring on the hull, either above or below the water-line. The analogy is immediately obvious. Certain mistakes are minor problems, which can easily be patched up. Others are not and would lead to catastrophe. It is a team leader's role to assess risk, to decide whether any potential mistakes are so serious that they cannot be allowed to go ahead or whether they can be let go because recovery would be easy and may be a useful learning experience for all involved. This means being a good judge of people and providing adequate support. It is indeed a risky strategy, but I believe it has paid dividends. Here are a few examples to help illustrate what I mean.

On several occasions I have let members of my church preach, without formal training or authorisation. This has not happened 'out of the blue' as they have already been involved in other areas of church life. It has not happened without providing others to work with them (sometimes myself, sometimes a trusted colleague). On one occasion it worked brilliantly, and I am encouraging the preacher to continue developing gifts in preaching and leading worship. On another occasion, it did not go so well, but that was only a single sermon—hardly a 'below the waterline' case, and there was still much goodwill towards the person in any case.

A church in which I was on the leadership team set up a group for women. It went all right to start with, but the group did not have the right combination of gifts and they began to struggle, so it was eventually decided to close it. This was a disappointment but hardly a disaster. On another occasion, the situation was very different. Someone wanted to start writing a blog and I agreed that they could. I kept an eye on it now and again. It was not particularly exciting, but nothing heretical either. Then someone saw a post that could have been very hurtful to another congregation member. I immediately asked for a meeting with the person, pointed out what the issue was and insisted the post was taken down. I then set firmer guidelines about what could be talked about in future.

I began preaching occasionally at the age of 16, in the context of a youth service. This was in itself a risk, as the other evening services at the time were all based on the Book of Common Prayer. The vicar stuck his neck out and gave us as the youth group one service a month to run and lead. We chose the music (within the limits of what the organist was prepared to play), we wrote the prayers, did drama and more. The congregation loved it (although, looking back, I doubt they understood it all, or even heard much of it). They were prepared to join in and to give us our lead, in order to encourage us. I now realise the risk the vicar was taking with us (quite literally on one exciting occasion, when a drama that involved powerful lights fused the electrics!) The church took other risks by allowing us to devise and run our own programme of activities, Bible studies and prayer groups. Three of us from that youth group went on to be ordained, another became a missionary, one a lay preacher and several more now play significant roles within their churches.

I have seen at first hand how cramping, how restricting, a lack of risk-taking can be. I once had a person on placement in my church who was exploring ordination. He had been leading the Sunday school at his church for many years but in terms of leading worship he had done no more than read the Gospel. The vicar was obviously keen to ensure that the quality of each and every service was the best, so this was all he was prepared to delegate. He was not even prepared to risk allowing this potential ordinand to lead the prayers. If we are to build people up, we need to give them responsibility. That does involve certain risks, but without that people will never grow.

You need to make an assessment of risk and be willing to step in and (to change the analogy) both to dig someone out of the hole they have made for themselves and then to start filling the hole. You cannot wash your hands of that person, let them take the blame or, even worse, criticise them (if you do, you will soon find sources of volunteers drying up). Another thing I was taught on the leadership course was that while you can delegate responsibility, you can never delegate accountability. It was US President Harry Truman who had a sign made for his desk in the Oval Office that said, 'The buck stops here.' He had seen it first on the desk of a prison governor. Each of us, at whatever level we lead, should be prepared to have that sign on our desk, in relation to those for whom we are responsible.

Trust

Leaders need to trust key volunteers who then model, as well as encourage, that trust elsewhere. Trust is crucial to teamwork. It is often slow to develop and easy to lose. Trust requires the effort of all the team members and the leader. To be trusted, you must be willing to trust others. Jesus trusted his followers. He trusted them enough to found his church, to become his Body, of which he remains the head. He continues to trust us.

Christ has no body now but yours,
No hands, no feet on earth but yours,
Yours are the eyes with which he looks compassion on this world.
Christ has no body now on earth but yours.
TERESA OF ÁVILA (1515–82)

Chapter 7

A word to leaders

Many people today are very concerned about their 'body image'. No longer is it just women who jump on the latest diet craze or go in for waxing (my eyes water at the very thought!) Although Western society as a whole has gone overboard on this, and the focus is becoming increasingly unhealthy, the idea of 'body image' is not a bad one when we are thinking about the Body of Christ. If we are all made in God's image, yet tainted by the Fall, should not members of his Church—those in whom God is working with his transforming power—be the closest the world has to his image (Ephesians 4:1; 2 Thessalonians 1:11; 2 Peter 1:10)? And should it not be church leaders who strive to attain the best, the most Christlike image (Matthew 20:25–26; Romans 12:8; Hebrews 13:7)? Now there's a challenge.

These thoughts came into my mind when I read that every church leader should aim to 'be a "supermodel"'.[48] That image raised a smile for me, and I hope it does for you too. Few of us would have any pretensions to being wildly attractive, but modelling good behaviour and good practice to the 'nth' degree is what all leaders should do.

There are many good leadership books around at the moment. My absolute favourite is Jim Collins' *From Good to Great*.[49] Collins is well known for his extensive research into leadership of major companies, and he has extended that research into what we in the UK would call the third sector. He sets out five levels of leadership, starting with a 'highly capable individual' and ending with level

5: 'executive'. The single thing that sets these level 5 leaders apart from the 'effective leader' of level 4 is humility.

In the social sectors, the level 5's compelling combination of personal humility and professional will is a key factor in creating legitimacy and influence. After all, why should those over whom you have no direct power give themselves over to a decision that is primarily about you?[50]

Such an attitude is crucial if the volunteers who work under you are going to respect you and give of their best for the cause for which you are all working. No one respects someone who is clearly out for empire-building. Sadly we do see this, even in the church: the choir leader who chooses complex music for worship that gives them the glory rather than God; or the person in charge of the flower rota who terrorises all, including the minister, who dare to suggest an arrangement might go anywhere other than exactly where they decree. I propose ways of tackling such people's behaviour if you are their minister in Chapter 11, but for now can I just say that those of us called to lead volunteers should be careful of our motives and how we use the powers we are given.

It is not always easy to exercise authority when you are working primarily with volunteers. As with ways to motivate, you have a very limited number of sanctions you can use. Jim Collins writes:

Whether they answer to a non-profit board… a set of trustees, a democratic religious organisation, an elected membership association or any number of other species of governance, social sector leaders face a complex and diffuse power map.[51]

What might this mean in terms of leading volunteer teams? What sort of things do we need to 'model' and how should we do that?

Model support

You should provide support for your volunteers to allow them to be both more effective and more fulfilled. This could mean that you may need to do more of the organising and the administrative tasks in order to support the volunteers (although if you are the church's minister with a large enough team, there will be, I would hope, a volunteer leader who is more directly involved who can take that on). Being a good leader will definitely mean making sure your volunteers have all the resources they need to carry out their tasks. It will mean arguing their case at whatever decision-making forum your church has. This includes:

- Firstly, money. A church's budget is a good indicator of its priorities. If you ask people to do your youth work, then give them an adequate budget. Too often I have come across an unspoken agreement in churches that seem to expect youth work in particular to be 'on the cheap', or even an expectation that the volunteers themselves will cover at least all the small costs. I have absolutely no doubt that some of my volunteers do indeed contribute out of their own pockets, that they do not claim all the expenses that they are rightly due. This is a generous attitude that I do not want to throw back in anyone's face. Yet it can lead to problems in the long term and is something I discourage. If a new volunteer takes over who cannot afford to subsidise the church's work (which not claiming expenses effectively is), then you immediately face a crisis. It is far better to ask people to put in a full expenses claim and, if they wish to cover the costs themselves, to do that by making a donation to the work of the church (which can then be gift-aided, so the church benefits even more). Only then will others in the church know the full costs of the work and make sure they budget appropriately.
- Secondly, space. Do they have the right size room(s) to cope with the numbers they have and activities they want to do? You

will rarely have all the facilities to meet the needs of all your groups perfectly, but you need to do the best you can. It is your role, as leader, to raise the issues with the 'powers that be' if space needs to be reallocated or even extended.

- Thirdly, equipment. This links to the point about budget, but it is also a matter of mindset. If you regularly need, say, specialist catering equipment that would make a group's work so much easier, then it is up to you to bring the matter forward and do what you can to ensure it is purchased, rather than leaving them to cope.

Model availability

Being available, accessible, is a key part of leadership behaviour. This is particularly important for the full-time professional leader. A new personal assistant was going through a bishop's diary. Every week, on the same afternoon, she saw 'emergency' written in. Puzzled, she asked him how he knew he would have an emergency at that time each week. 'I don't,' he replied, 'but I know that I will have one some time, and I want to make sure I have space in my diary to rearrange things so that I can respond.'

This is a story I often repeat as advice, yet I struggle to follow that advice myself. It is not always easy, but I try as hard as I can to keep enough space in my diary to make an appointment with someone who wants one within a few days, if not immediately. This approach has come from personal experience, when I have tried to book appointments with someone, even in a local church situation, only to be told the earliest slot is three (or more) weeks away. I do not think that is acceptable and have worked hard to ensure that I can always see people for urgent matters as soon as possible. A real emergency, of course, is different, and means you need to drop everything.

Without in any way wanting to expose more leaders to the

possibility of burnout (even Jesus was not always available, and he took time away—see Luke 5:15–16), I suggest that highly defined boundaries are generally not helpful for leaders. Perhaps the example of 'going the extra mile' (Matthew 5:41) is not exactly analogous, but the whole context of that section of the Beatitudes is one of doing above and beyond what is expected or even demanded by the Law. Any kind of behaviour by the leader that is legalistic in terms of contract expectations is not going to encourage those who give their time freely.

Giving time, real adequate time, to volunteers will most certainly cut into your own ministry, but it is crucial. The maths is simple. Investing time in several others to help them develop will eventually create more time for ministry overall. I think of the vicar with whom three of us were placed while we were training. Every Monday afternoon we met together so that he could feed back to us how things had gone on Sunday. He did this in a particularly helpful way, but it was the fact that he gave us time that was important in itself. It took a couple of hours out of each week, but I like to think that his investment has paid off for the wider church. And each of the three of us now has that model for our own ministry, which leads neatly to my next point.

Modelling through mentoring

A recent sermon series in our church looked at leadership by preaching through 1 Timothy, which is a letter by a senior, well-experienced leader giving advice to a more junior one. To ensure that people did not think I was just aiming the series at those in church with 'official' leadership positions, I emphasised that we almost all had opportunities to exercise leadership at some level. It was also a call for members of the congregation to pray for those of us who lead. Paul looks at a number of very practical issues— doctrine, sexual ethics, praying for those in authority, dress and behaviour, relationships at work, money, as well as the kind of character leaders in a church should have. But Timothy does not only figure in the letters Paul wrote to him. We can learn about building up others through mentoring from the way Paul worked with him.

- **Take people with us.** Paul first met Timothy in Derbe (Acts 16:1) and immediately saw potential in him. Timothy had a good reputation locally, so Paul decided to take him along with him. Timothy would have had the opportunity to watch and learn, to see what sort of example of ministry and of leadership Paul was setting. This was also the pattern of Jesus—choosing the Twelve out of the wider group to be especially close, and Peter, James and John to be closer still. How much do you do this? How often do you take someone with you when you do a talk, a pastoral visit, or attend a conference? How often do you let them work with you as you prepare a service or to lead a group?
- **Give others responsibility.** There came a point, again as with Jesus and the disciples, where Paul decided to let Timothy take on more (1 Corinthians 4:17). The Anglican Church has a system of curates, who come from college to receive a few years 'hands on' training with an experienced minister. When I was in that position and compared notes with a friend, six months in, our experiences were vastly different. In regards to funerals for example: he had spent six months accompanying his vicar to funerals and been allowed to do nothing more than a reading, while I had conducted 15 complete funerals, including all the preparatory visits.
- **Continuing support.** We do not hear anything about Paul's 'supervision sessions' with Timothy, although we do get a snippet of Jesus with his disciples (Luke 10:17–19). As well as giving volunteers responsibility, it is essential to provide continuing support, which is very time intensive but an investment for the future. I am currently supporting three people through Reader

training. For each I am making space for one-to-one sessions, spend time looking through written work and talking through issues. In due course they will be leading and preaching more regularly, thus freeing me to do other work. At least that is the case with two of them. The third is a member of another church. I will never gain any personal return on my investment here, but the wider church of God will. That was clearly Paul's motivation.

- **Pray for them.** Paul says, 'I constantly remember you in my prayers' (2 Timothy 1:3). We need to pray for people while they are with us, and continue to do so once they have moved on to their own ministry.

- **Working in pairs.** Even when Timothy was ready to work without supervision Paul did not leave him completely on his own, certainly not at first. We hear of him with Silas (Acts 17:14–15; 18:5) and Erastus (19:22). Paul also continued to work closely with Timothy himself. Timothy appears frequently alongside Paul and on several occasions Silas was there too (2 Corinthians 1:19; 1 Thessalonians 1:1; 2 Thessalonians 1:1). Paul clearly believed in teamwork.

- **Prepare others with whom your trainee is going to work.** Paul did not just send Timothy to work with a church unannounced but he sent him with a glowing reference (1 Corinthians 4:17; 16:10). I have written many references in my time. If you are not sent such background, it is up to you, as a responsible leader, to do the research. Every now and again I get offers of someone to speak to groups or general offers of help but I never simply pass them straight on. If I think a person might be able to help, I will do what I can to 'check them out'. That is not a lack of trust but a sensible precaution of a responsible leader.

All this is time-intensive, and we have only so much time to give. Sometimes we have to be selective in who we mentor and encourage. We do not know exactly what Paul saw in Timothy that encouraged him to take him on as a trainee leader, but we do know why he did not take on Mark (Acts 15:36–41) about whom he had some concerns. Paul took on Silas instead, another of his protégés. We have to be realistic. On the other hand, the more people we train up, the more leaders there are to whom we can delegate, the wider the circle of those in ministry becomes and the more work gets done.

The analogy I would use for mentoring is not so much that of one of those Domino toppling contests, in which one knocks another, which knocks another, and so on. It is more that of a nuclear reaction, with one atom splitting and setting off two, two setting off four, and so on. Or perhaps, fitting even better with the theme of this book, we can think of a single fertilised egg cell that becomes two, then four, then eight and so on, until a foetus is formed, and eventually, one day, the whole process starts again.

A small aside: Barnabas took on Mark because Paul did not want to. Yet, as a result of Barnabas' input, Mark flourished, and Paul realised this and came to rely on him (2 Timothy 4:11). Others will love working with those you find very frustrating. You need a variety of mentors to bring out the best in the whole Body. Make sure you do not discount people too quickly just because you do not warm to them. They will have talents worth developing too. Mentoring those who have the skills to mentor others in turn may be aiming for perfection (but then again, why not?) and is easier in a larger church, where you have more people to choose from. You might simply be grateful to find someone to get an immediate job done, but keep looking for opportunities to take all your volunteers on to the next stage. Only then will you get real and sustained growth in the individual, and thus in the Body as a whole.

Model giving away

Be prepared to give up some of the 'hands on' work that you enjoy so much. Clergy can be quite poor at delegation, although this is not an exclusively clerical trait. We either enjoy something too much or know we are better at it than most and do not want to see work done poorly! Others are happy to give away small areas of service, such as allowing children to take a collection or gather up hymn books, which can be easily controlled (and come with a high 'Ah' factor) but find it more difficult to allow other adults (who might take a different approach) to exercise real responsibility. I have seen clergy asking members to do a job—often one taking a lot of time—while still keeping a close eye on them and even rejecting or redoing the task when the work has been finished. And I have seen this cause major, although thankfully not irreconcilable, conflict.

Because I have some experience in magazine design, I offered to step in to produce an issue of our magazine when the regular editor could not. Not only did this give me a lot more respect for the work she puts into each edition, but it also made me realise that I would not want to do it more often. Yes, I can do it, but it is far better to find someone else to train and encourage. Likewise I can produce a reasonable presentation for use in services. I know what wire goes where and I can operate the software. Very occasionally I will do this, but if I were to do it week by week, I would not be allowing others to use their gifts.

Then, to take a quite different area of church life, I love preaching. I have been taught that preaching is a key element of a minister's role, and I believe I have the gifts to do it reasonably well. Yet there are an increasing number of weeks when I do not get to preach the sermon. That is because I wish to encourage others who feel a calling to preach to develop their gifts in this area. It is the same with leading worship. I believe that is one of my gifts, but much of our church worship is led by others.

There is another very good reason to delegate work. To avoid getting pulled in too many directions, you will need to limit those things for which you have 'hands on' responsibility. Moses was recommended to provide leaders at different levels by his father-in-law, Jethro (Exodus 18:24–26) because 'the work is too heavy for you; you cannot handle it alone' (v. 18). Nehemiah brought a great team of volunteers together (Nehemiah 3). Even Jesus sometimes stepped back and let the disciples take charge (for example, Luke 10:1–24), although sometimes he had to step back in (see Matthew 17:14–18).

If I am to develop others, I must do less myself. I must put more of my time into training, encouraging, reflecting with them afterwards. It is really good for you to give up something you love and are good at, in order to see others blossom.

If Paul had stuck with what he enjoyed and did very well rather than training others, the church would not have flourished as it did. Jesus sent the Twelve, and the Seventy, off to do the two things he was certainly better at—preaching and healing—even when at times they failed (Mark 9:28–29). Once others are trained, let go. Stepping back and, even more so, stepping down is not easy. Someone who once did a great deal of work in a church was unhappy at the idea of relinquishing her role of service and becoming a 'pew filler'. Now I hate that word, because I believe passionately that there should be no such thing, that everyone has gifts to use. I told this person so, saying she would remain a valued member of the church, even if no longer doing quite so much. If we do not step back, then others will not step forward to offer their gifts and we end up with 'pew fillers'. The church will then be less effective than it might be, and each person less fulfilled, less whole than they could be.

Of course there will be others who are able to do what you can, and better. You need to allow that too, without fearing you will be outshone. Preventing them from using their gifts does not just limit them but limits the ministry of the whole church. Some musical clergy insist on choosing all the music for services rather than allowing the organist or choir leader to do so. Some are so good at technology that they keep responsibility for it when other, perfectly competent people could do so.

One vicar I knew, who loved using cartoon illustrations, produced some excruciatingly bad drawings—until someone in the congregation volunteered to create them for him, much to everyone's relief. It also meant that a gift that might have otherwise remained unused was developed and the congregation member was affirmed and built up and went on to do much more within the church.

Ultimately, people are built up by believing they are doing something truly valuable for God. This generally involves doing something truly valuable for others—and we must allow them to do so. As leaders we should model the truth that the place will not fall to pieces without us. 'Help' is a key word: you must offer it and ask for it.

Model trust

The ultimate gift to give to your congregation is to work yourself out of a job—to find new people not just to replace others who step down but to replace you. Paul is not precious about keeping all control to himself, provided he trusted the others: 'What, after all, is Apollos? And what is Paul? Only servants, through whom you came to believe—as the Lord has assigned to each his task... neither the one who plants nor the one who waters is anything, but only God, who makes things grow... we are fellow workers in God's service' (1 Corinthians 3:5, 7, 9).

The youth worker our church employed worked very hard with his team of volunteers to find someone else, a volunteer, to take over his role when he left. In the Anglican Church, a key lay leadership role is that of the churchwarden. Most churches have two. The maximum length they can serve, in normal circumstances, is six years, so it is not long before another person is required. Some churches have a deputy warden system to train up the next churchwarden.

At one small church the Elders used to do everything. This went far beyond their official responsibilities (including putting out the rubbish bins and the parking cones) and was done out of the best of intentions, from a real servant heart. The situation continued for many years, as successive Elders simply took on the growing list of responsibilities without challenging it. It was okay for the first changeover, and not too bad for the next. The problem was that when the time came for those Elders in turn to hand over their responsibilities, the rest of the congregation had been 'trained' out of thinking that all these small things might be their responsibility. They just assumed that someone else would do those jobs, rather than stepping forward and offering help. In time others did step forward but it had led to a crisis that need not have arisen in the first place, due to the encouragement of a culture in which everyone thought someone else would take charge.

If you do not delegate and do not encourage others, then you will create problems because you will send out a signal that you do not trust your volunteers. When you do delegate, step back and let people get on with it. Do not 'micro-manage' and trust that your way is unlikely to be the only way, and it might not even be the best! If you do not trust your volunteers (and if you don't, ask yourself why) then do not delegate in the first place. It is equally important that your volunteers know they can trust you. A lack of trust is bad enough in the world of work, but in a volunteer situation it is truly disastrous. And, with younger generations in particular, trust of leaders must be earned, because it does not come automatically with a position. It can easily be lost and, once lost, it is very hard to regain.

Model good decision-making

This means sharing decision-making. We do not see this aspect in Jesus' ministry (although he did delegate considerable authority to the disciples—see, for example, Matthew 10:5–20). In doing so, he built them up for their future responsibilities. Paul could be quite autocratic at times (see Acts 15:28; 1 Corinthians 11:16), but one can normally find very specific or spiritual reasons for this. We can see shared leadership in action elsewhere in the early church (Acts 6:2–5; 15:25–27). I have already argued that leadership of a team does not mean you should make all the decisions.

It does mean being prepared to make the hard decisions. If in the end you simply cannot find anyone to take on a role, you have to accept that it cannot be done at this time. This is so important that I will return to it in Chapter 11.

Model a new way of thinking

I find the idea of 'Emotional Intelligence' (as popularised by Daniel Goleman)[52] particularly helpful when thinking of the kind of leader I need to be. At root this is a general awareness that the emotional side of people is crucially important. This is especially true when you are dealing with volunteers, because emotions are key to satisfaction and motivation, and the satisfaction the work itself offers is the only 'reward' we have to offer.

Unlike in the world of employment, where people can be offered more pay, longer holidays or other incentives, volunteers work for 'job satisfaction' alone. Interestingly, increased financial rewards have been found to have only limited value in motivating people at work. In the long term the more personal needs and feelings are most important, and we can do just as well with these for our volunteers.

What does it mean to lead volunteers with Emotional Intelligence? It is about being aware of their emotional needs and drivers, as well as your own. It is about feeling, not just thinking, about treating people as you would like to be treated, about forgiveness and forbearance. Is this beginning to sound familiar?

'Love your neighbour as yourself.' (Mark 12:31)

'For the mouth speaks what the heart is full of.' (Luke 6:45)

'Even if they sin against you seven times in a day and seven times come back to you saying "I repent," you must forgive them.' (Luke 17:4)

It is hardly surprising that Jesus should be acting as the classic Emotionally Intelligent leader, 2000 years before the theory was devised. Leading in this way is not easy, but it is crucial. Volunteers who are not positively motivated by those who lead them will eventually take their valuable skills and time elsewhere. I can think of many examples of frequently highly gifted and committed people, have been hugely put upon and little appreciated. They moved to other churches and organisations where they gave as much, if not more, but where they felt their contribution was better recognised. It was not that they sought recognition or 'kudos', but they did appreciate a leader who appreciated what they did and supported them. The lack of Emotional Intelligence in a leader can bring huge anguish for individuals and significant loss to the organisation. Goleman has a phrase for this as well: 'toxic leadership'.[53] In a 'toxic' atmosphere, we lose the goodwill of volunteers. The group is then far less likely to be able to recruit new volunteers, let alone retain existing ones. I have seen this happen in secular and Christian organisations alike. Leaders do not set out to be toxic, but through a lack of emotional awareness they have this effect.

There is not an absolute link between Emotional Intelligence and humility, but I would argue for a close relationship between them, and that both are crucial when you are leading volunteers, whether as a paid professional or as a volunteer leader.[54] And a vital leadership role, however small or large the group you are leading, is to set the culture (at its simplest defined as 'the way we do things around here'). Others in the group will follow the lead you set. Modelling the right outlook in the way I have suggested above are all important aspects of setting a positive culture.

Chapter 8

The professional problem

When churches reach a certain size, they often want to employ staff to do some of the work previously done by volunteers. Scan the Christian magazines, papers and websites and you will see plenty of adverts for youth and children's workers, community workers, evangelists, administrators, musicians and, of course, ministers. As one of the latter I feel that there are certain advantages in having at least one or two professionals among the church staff! As early as the church in Corinth there were clearly issues around the matter of payment for Christian work (1 Corinthians 9). The point of this chapter is not to argue the advantages and disadvantages of professional staff, but to reflect on the kind of issues that can arise between professionals and volunteers and how best to deal with them. Whether you have just a single professional, or a larger number, it is vital to have the relationships right.

'It's all about relationships'

Somebody said to me about church life: 'It's basically all about relationships.' It is not about processes, systems or strategies, however important they seem. Whatever the task, whatever the size or scope of the church or organisation, the relationships are fundamental. A number of charities have run into problems when a seemingly logical 'improved' way of operating, devised by chief executives and professional staff, has been imposed on local groups composed entirely of volunteers. It would not be too strong to say that, occasionally, 'all hell has broken loose'.

Those of us who are paid to work for a church have a special obligation to make sure we understand the needs and motivations of 'amateurs', those who do it purely 'for the love of it', and to relate to them with great care and consideration, never taking anyone for granted. It is not just because this is the right thing to do. An Urban Institute report shows that proper involvement, care and appreciation of volunteers produces significant benefits for charities and, important as paid staff can be, it is equally important to continue to involve the largest possible numbers of volunteers.[55] Organisations with a high volunteer-to-paid staff ratio (as the case with most churches) report increased benefits, regardless of their size and budget. As the report says on page 1, 'Resources are important, but money alone cannot buy benefits from volunteers.'

You cannot legislate for good relationships but, just like 'good fences make good neighbours', so good staff/volunteer relationships begin with good management practices, ways that are respectful, transparently fair and reasonable.

The 'M' word

I have used the word 'leadership' throughout the previous chapter because to some people 'management' smacks of close control. They feel that leadership is good and biblical and management is bad and worldly. They fear aping the business world with its target-driven processes, but this does not have to be the case. Good management techniques work in any situation. Interestingly, there was a similar debate in secular literature on the subject, but people have generally moved beyond this now. Jim Collins' research shows how the very same principles that make certain businesses 'great' work equally well for the charity sector.

Rather than using practices and techniques to bend people to your will in some Machiavellian way, good management is basically about good working relationships. A good professional manager of volunteers is a good listener, with empathy and understanding, and building honesty into their relationship. If the person doing the managing respects the volunteers then the volunteers will respect them. This is not rocket science but common sense. So why are there so many relationship problems in volunteer teams?

Charles Handy, who has written a standard work in this field, argues a strong case for the absolute necessity of good management:

Reject management and all its ways and you invite not only the tyranny of democracy but two other perils of voluntarism: strategic delinquency and the servant syndrome, both of which can end up by abusing individuals and organisations.[56]

This is especially true at times of change. Democracy is great (for example, I have just surveyed everyone in my church about the time for our services) but there are times when the variety of opinions is so considerable, or the situation so complex, that a smaller, better informed group or an individual needs to decide the way forward. Strategy is important but can have its limitations; different people can have widely differing views of where to go in the shorter and longer term. Again, good management of expectations and the process is vital. I will return to the third issue shortly.

Making decisions

Most churches have at least one 'professional' in the staff team. This, at its root, simply means that you, if you are the professional, are paid for your time, and others are not. It does not mean that you necessarily know more or have more skills or experience. It definitely does not mean that you are the one who should make all the decisions, even if your church puts the responsibility for those decisions on your shoulders. Are you always clearly 'in charge', always chairing the meetings, always coming up with the ideas and expecting others to implement them? If so, I suggest you think again. This may have worked in the past, but it is no longer adequate. Continue and you simply will not get younger volunteers to join you.

Remember: a volunteer is not 'just' a volunteer. They are a whole person with a whole raft of skills and life experience. They may have significant expertise in a field that bears directly on the decision in hand, which it would be foolish to ignore—such as strategic planning, project management, financial matters, people management and indeed leadership itself. If a qualified volunteer offers advice in this area, listen carefully. If you are the expert, offer advice circumspectly. Rather than saying, 'Here is a new system, please follow it,' talk about it with your team first and see what they think. I have lost count of the times I have made a great (to me) suggestion to my volunteer team, only to have a lukewarm reception or a flat 'we don't think that's a good idea'. If this happens *every* time you make a suggestion, then you are clearly in the wrong role. Having said that, you should expect your ideas to attract a genuine, even robust response that will help to improve them. No one is perfect and no one gets it right all the time, not even a 'professional'. To listen graciously and to be prepared to change your mind and to see another point of view will only increase the respect your team have for you, and how much they are prepared to do for you. Brother Tom, from Hilfield Priory, said:

If you believe that God works through all of us, it behoves you to live out this truth. One way of doing this is to treat every conversation with a spirit of anticipation, expecting to hear how God is working through them and eagerly wanting to make sense of what he is saying to us, through them.[57]

Getting things right is not always the most important thing. I still vividly remember a time when I was trying to put a volunteer youth leader straight about the rules of a game he was leading. I wanted it to be played correctly; he saw it as interfering. It was only after he'd walked away that I realised that allowing him leadership responsibility was more important than getting the rules right. What you say and do may have unforeseen effects on those with less confidence or with bad experiences of authority in the past.

Using professionals can stop volunteering altogether

On a recent trip to Sweden, where churches employ many professionals (staff teams of 30 to 50, including ministers, social workers, musicians and administrators are not uncommon), I heard the frustrations of those volunteers who are faced with so many professionals that they cannot use their skills. The professionals too admitted that they knew people wanted to volunteer, but they struggled to find work for them to do. They could see how this was detrimental to the growth of their church members as individuals, and their church as a whole.

However many paid staff you do or do not have, it is important to develop the right thinking and attitudes across the church. For example, it is not 'the minister' (or, failing that, the next best thing, her assistant) who should do all the hospital visiting, pastoral visiting, funeral follow-ups, baptism visits and so on. This is simply impossible, apart from churches with very small congregations. It may be the expectation of the congregation that needs to be worked on. It may also be the attitude of the paid staff, who may well like to be seen as all-competent and pretty much omnipresent.

Some church congregations expect paid staff to do most of the work, so that those who pay their wages can have an easier life! Whenever I have come across that attitude, it has been little less than disastrous. I think sometimes people regard professionals in the church in the way they regard skilled workers, from car mechanics and plumbers through to doctors and lawyers. You expect such professionals to perform a service for you, as ministers are expected to do all the visiting, evangelism and service leading. Rather than being the 'jack of all trades' or 'dogsbody', however, ministers and other professionals in the church should aim to have a role more akin to that of a theatre or film director. They have their own skills and their own role, central to which is to guide and get the best out of each and every individual actor.

A local group of churches employed a youth worker. The job description was clear: to train, encourage and build a team of volunteers to run a series of youth groups. The person appointed was to work alongside this team, indeed to lead it. When the youth worker arrived, she found a predominant attitude that now the churches had 'a professional', others could take a back seat. People expected her to do just about everything, and she found it hard to draw in enough helpers to run all that was expected. Things were made worse when the lead minister for the project, who had had the original vision, left. Soon after that the youth worker left too, because she no longer had adequate support. There was no one else who would speak for her in the decision-making bodies. The whole scheme was no longer viable but, to be honest, it never had been.

What issues were involved here? For a start, it seemed that the proposal had not been truly 'owned' by all the church ministers, let alone the congregations, but rather that one person's enthusiasm had driven it through. There was also clearly a difference in expectations, which indeed varied from church to church. There was a lack of communication about the scope of the new role and how it would relate to what had already been provided. When the situation began to go wrong, which it did from an early stage of the process, the churches' leadership did not take proper action. The youth worker herself was not listened to nor were her concerns reflected on. It does not have to be like that. In another church a youth worker was employed and great things happened. Young people enjoyed themselves and more were drawn in.[58] As with so many activities, what matters is not what you do but how you do it (and in both of these cases, how thoroughly you prepare for it).

Getting your hands dirty

Equally, paid staff sometimes expect volunteers to do all the 'dirty work' and keep the exciting stuff to themselves. That is no better than the other way round. There should be mutual respect, mutual appreciation and mutual service.

Once again we can look back to Jesus. 'No one wanted to be considered the least. Then Jesus took a towel and a basin and so redefined greatness.'[59] Long before the events of the Last Supper (John 13:2–17) Jesus was already modelling and teaching that sort of leadership: 'Whoever wants to become great among you must be your servant... the Son of Man did not come to be served, but to serve.' (Matthew 20:26–28). The pattern Jesus set is one of serving those you lead.[60]

As with Jesus and his bowl of water and towel, the effect of the leader cleaning the tables or grabbing the broom to sweep up cannot be underestimated, for example: 'I spent a morning cleaning the church, as the interns were doing, just mucking in with others.' I have known leaders in many organisations who have gained significant credit among those whom they lead for actions as simple as moving a few chairs or grabbing a tea towel or making the tea for the team. Such behaviour helps break down any idea of 'us and them', any suggestion that the leader's time is more valuable than theirs, that certain activities are OK for volunteers but beneath those who lead them.

We need to be careful, though. Being a servant-leader isn't all about the menial but about far deeper issues than that. If it stops there, it can cause real problems and leads to 'servant syndrome'. Charles Handy is strongly against the idea that everyone must do all his or her own menial work. To be a servant leader does *not* mean you refuse to let other do things for you. In many organisations, especially perhaps churches, the simple but time-consuming tasks are exactly what volunteers can do, to great effect. Handy's second point about 'servant syndrome' is the 'constant need to respond', not just to be available but to be around constantly as the one who fixes everything. This is all too common and is not only detrimental to the leader, leading to burnout and worse, but is not actually helpful or honouring to the volunteer. If a leader is always stepping in to do what a volunteer has signed up to do, it can be highly demotivating for the volunteer.

Be aware that different expectations can exist between paid staff and volunteers, which may cause tensions. Perhaps volunteers have lots of ideas but little time. Are there issues of professional pride versus the attitude, 'We'll give it a go—that's good enough'? Or, alternatively, between volunteer passion versus 'These are my hours and I'm sticking to them'? There are clergy who expect others, already busy, to volunteer to run activities, such as socials, which they themselves do not attend; staff workers who do not do anything, ever, on their days off; and others who refuse to be contacted out of office hours, even in an emergency. What does that say to the volunteers you ring up at home, to those whom you ask to change their plans to do something extra or to step in at the last minute?

A friend of mine at college insisted that when they moved into a parish they would only ever work a two-session day (in other words, not morning, afternoon and evening). He stuck to this and it became part of his reputation, and not the most positive part.

Churches all too easily assume that paid staff will be able to work well with volunteers but that is not necessarily the case. Staff will need training in this area as much as in any other. Any good management or leadership training should cover the basics of dealing with people, and I have found that the best practices work well with any group, paid or not. What is important is to ensure that some training, some introduction to the area, is given.[61]

If you are a professional new to working with volunteers, find a more experienced mentor, perhaps asking for this as part of your induction. I have run regular supervision sessions with the three professional staff who have come to our church straight from college or on placement. We tackled a variety of people-oriented issues and thought through what had gone well or what not so well.

It is also important to encourage senior staff to have direct contact with volunteers in working situations, not just in meetings. An Australian Archbishop spends a couple of weeks each year leading a small group of young people to Sudan. His aim is not only to give them an experience of a different culture and way of 'being church' but also to let them spend time with him, seeing how he behaves at first hand. To him encouraging new young leaders is a key part of his ministry.

The behaviour of the senior leader/leadership team is crucial. The example they set, good or bad, will filter down (especially the bad). Volunteers today demand, whether explicitly or not, more time and better management practices from those who lead them. They respond to appraisals (formal or not), mentoring, regular reviews, 'volunteer agreements'. Gen X and Y are used to these in their working life and they expect their leaders, even in voluntary situations, to be professional. Volunteers need a particular style of manager, one who will nurture and lead, empower, inspire, support, not one who will be carping and critical, quick to come down on any minor slip ups. Perhaps above all, they need one who communicates well.

Communicate, communicate, communicate

Communication is absolutely crucial to any relationship. In any normal human body there are many, many, different messages going around, both electrical and chemical. Without a continual two-way 'conversation' between different parts, the body could not work. The way we walk, for example, involves some very fine communication indeed, with message and response between muscle, eyes, balance system, nerves and brain, time and time again. The Body of Christ needs an equal amount of good communication.

The more staff and more volunteers you have, the more important good communication becomes. Make sure paid staff keep volunteers 'in the loop'. This can happen only if communication between staff is good too. One volunteer was both confused and upset when she discovered, via a person she was working with, that a 'client' had been given different information from one member of staff than she herself had about some quite significant matters. There was high potential for embarrassment as well as a poor reputation for the church. Involve volunteers fully in discussions, meetings and social gatherings, which includes something as basic as copying them into group emails.

Talking of email, it is a brilliant communication tool but one with significant limitations. Over the years I have seen some very difficult situations caused through careless use of language in emails. And in these days of texts, Facebook, Twitter and other social media, much of what I say here about email refers to these forms of communication too. Here are a few suggested 'do's and don't's' to get you thinking:

- Use it to pass on information. It is a great tool for disseminating facts and figures, reports and minutes, announcing events, and so on. People can copy and paste text and file information easily. If you want to point people to a website, you can do this straight from an email.
- Use it to ask people. I would not suggest you do this regularly, and only when you already have a good relationship with the person, but it can be less threatening to ask this way than a face-to-face 'Will you do this?', or a phone call, as it gives them time to reflect and check the diary.

- Take care with the tone. An email is more like a transcribed phone call than a letter, and unlike with a phone call, you are lacking one crucial carrier of information: the tone of voice. You can use '!' and ':-)' to help (although do not overuse them). I suggest avoiding 'text speak' such as 'LOL' (which, as some rather important people have found out to their cost, can mean both 'Laugh out Loud' and 'Lots of Love'). And DO NOT EVER use all capitals, as it 'sounds' like shouting.
- Beware of the instant reply. Think to yourself—are you clear you have understood what the sender is saying? Do you need any further information? Do you need time to think more carefully rather than offer a gut reaction? Should you consult anyone else first? When you are confronted with dozens of emails for reply, short, rapid responses are very tempting. The chances are that such emails will just draw a further question or comment. It may be an old proverb but 'more haste, less speed' could have been invented for the internet age.
- Always reread before sending. Think carefully whether your words are completely clear. And beware of 'auto-correct' and predictive text features. Once I texted someone asking whether they had 'a lift yet' and was horrified to reread, after sending it, that what had gone was 'have you got a life yet?' A rapid correction was sent!
- Do not always reply to an email with an email. It is very easy for the heat of an email conversation to ratchet up rapidly. Do not let yourself get drawn into this kind of conversation. Reach for the phone; make an appointment to see them.
- Archive conversations. Email (and social media) provides a trail, a 'thread' to which you can refer back, to remind yourself what all parties have said. In an increasingly complex and litigious world this can be very useful.
- A useful reminder. Perhaps it is just me, but if someone asks me to do something as they leave a church service and I say 'yes, of course', I may just forget after the next half dozen conversations.

These days I either respond, 'Certainly, but would you mind dropping me an email to remind me?', or make a note on my smartphone, which is then imported into my email software.

- Remember that an email can be easily forwarded. How many emails have you received because the sender has hit the 'reply all' rather than the 'reply' button? Mostly it is just annoying, but I have certainly received messages I should not have had. Leaving that problem aside, anything you send can easily be forwarded to someone else outside the original group. If you want to avoid having your emails forwarded to a person's many friends, with a comment like 'Do you see what he said to me...!' added in front, then avoid making the kind of messages that could not be forwarded. Indeed be very circumspect about comments you make in an email, especially observations to one volunteer about others.

- Make good use of the Bcc box. Unless the group you are emailing already know each other or need to reply to all, you should use the Bcc box for all addresses, so as not to pass on private email addresses to the other recipients.

- A quick 'thank you'. Certainly not the only, or even the best method (see Chapter 10), but probably the most immediate, which has a value in itself. You could of course use a text or a phone call instead. With this, as with any other use of email, pause and think for a moment whether an email is best, or whether some other way would be better.

- Do not use it for anything really urgent. You do not know whether it has been read. Emails are also easy to ignore, and do not 'jump out' at you. Text is likely to be better but for a really urgent response a phone call is still best.

- Do not deliver bad news by email. You will have no doubt heard some horror stories of people who have heard they have been made redundant via email or text. Take care you do not pass on bad news to your volunteers in a similar way. Don't hide behind email but do it in person.

Still a volunteer at heart

If you are paid to work for the church ask yourself these questions:

- Are you living what you are asking others to do?
- What is your own record of volunteering?
- Are you still an 'amateur' too? Loving the job and the people?

Aiming to retain the amateur or volunteer mentality yourself makes a huge difference. And what's the best way to do that? Volunteer yourself, of course: 'I only get paid for eight hours, the rest is voluntary... I'm pretty much fulltime, really.' 'Forty hours is what I have to do and beyond that it is more my choice, what I love doing. It keeps me fresh.' If you are paid staff, do you work extra hours for the project or organisation for which you are responsible, or perhaps for some other cause?

Professionals bring much to a church who can afford to employ them, as do volunteers. Having both is simply another aspect of the Body. To end this chapter where we began—let us do all we can to make sure relationships between them are right.

Chapter 9

Practicalities

We've already thought about how the human body is an amazing thing. All the complex processes needed for health and growth just happen, unconsciously. You breathe without thinking. If you get a cut or an infection, the body's defences kick in without your having to do anything. The body does not come with a thick instruction manual that you need to know backwards. Good processes are just as important for the Body of Christ but, sadly, these do not come automatically. They need to be learnt and followed carefully.

So often we groan when 'red tape' is mentioned, and we may feel that 'we used to manage without all this'. Yes, we did, but times have changed. It is not just that we are living in a more litigious culture, although it would be foolish not to bear this in mind, but that we have a responsibility to all those we serve, including our own volunteers. It is part of our duty of care to follow good practice, to have good policies; to carry out good risk assessments and so on.

The basics

Volunteering England has produced a useful Code of Practice for volunteers themselves,[62] interestingly in response to a 'red tape taskforce' chaired by Lord Hodgson called 'Unshackling Good Neighbours'.[63] This is a useful code that might be worth passing around your volunteers, but it is also a good guide for the basics that we should be aware of in terms of reducing risk:

1. Take care in whatever you do. Act reasonably and follow the rest of these guidelines.
2. Think about your safety and the safety of others around you. Take time to think about the risks something could pose to you and others. If there is a risk, think about how you can reduce it.
3. Involve other people. Before you do something, think about who else it might involve or affect. If you have noticed that something needs doing, others may have too. By talking about it with others, you are more likely both to identify potential problems and to be able to solve them.
4. Ask for help and information. If something is challenging, where might you go for help? If you have concerns about health and safety, ask someone outside the organisation, such as Citizens Advice Bureau.
5. Be clear about what you are and are not responsible for. Check out the myths and the law.
6. Check your existing insurance policies to see what you are covered for. Home insurance may well cover a range of activities for individual volunteers.
7. If you are volunteering for an organisation, you are probably covered by their insurance. There should be no 'probably' for a responsible Christian organisation. Churches need a good employee and volunteer insurance, alongside public liability.

Policies and procedures

Policies you may want to consider include:

- Safeguarding
- Health & safety
- Complaints
- Handling money/expenses

- Grievance
- Disciplinary

The first two are not optional, and the others are useful to have too. Try to keep them simple, but clear. You do not need to work them up from scratch as there are many good examples and templates freely available.[64]

Safeguarding

Make sure you are up to date in this area. Many people still talk about 'child protection', but although this is a key part, it is now also extended to include vulnerable adults. If you are part of a larger group of churches, you will almost certainly find they will have access to specialist staff. If you are not, the Churches' Child Protection Advisory Service is a good place to start.[65]

Risk Assessment and risk management

I moan as much as anyone about today's 'health and safety' obsessed culture but, leaving aside the fact that certain things are legal requirements these days and will affect insurance, ensuring that volunteers and those they serve have a safe working environment is important. Legislation on this is changing all the time, so it is worth having someone in your church whose responsibilities include keeping up to date in such matters. You may well find that church members who work in industry, teaching or the various social care professions will already be well informed in their work roles, so make sure you make full use of their expertise.

There are certain procedures that *must* be carried out, such as a proper risk assessment for insurance purposes. There are other practices that are *advisable*, for example, having two people to count money after services. Money is generally a sensitive issue, and one where care is needed.

Expenses

Basic procedures should be in place. We tend to trust people, but having such a simple policy as payment against receipts or record of mileage saves any risk of doubt. It is not good for your group nor fair to the people involved, to do otherwise.

As already mentioned, part of respecting people and not taking them for granted is having an adequate budget for expenses and making it clear that people should claim them. Not only is it simply the right thing to do but it also helps you to set a realistic budget overall. Does your youth work really cost only £250 per year as your church budget says, or is it closer to £1000 because your volunteers are picking up the rest of the costs? If they feel this is expected, it could cause resentment, but it is not good for the church either.

Role descriptions

'How do you fancy helping out with the youth group on Friday night?' That's a fairly traditional way of recruiting a volunteer. Of course *you* know exactly what you mean by that, but what might be going through the prospective volunteer's head? 'Oh no, does that mean I have to wear jeans and be prepared to play silly games?', 'How much of my time will that take?', 'I'd be happy to make the coffee and tidy up, but they probably want more than that.', 'Well, I guess I wouldn't mind doing it for six months, but I know that Martin has been doing it for at least six years, so I'd better say no, in case I get sucked in.'

Before you approach people it is a good idea to have something very specific in mind. Treasurer—are they responsible for collecting subs and buying coffee or for an annual budget of £50,000? Cleaner—that mean the whole building on your own every week? Or being one of a team of three on a fortnightly rota? What preparation might be required? This is important, because if the two hours each week is likely to require a further three hours preparation time, your volunteer needs to know that.

Emlyn Williams makes the very good point that a role description that is too generic can be off-putting for some.[66] Spell out, for example, that the youth work request means making the tea, designing posters and running the tuck shop and that it does *not* (necessarily) mean organising games or making a fool of yourself in a drama (and if it does mean this, say so). By being more specific, you are more likely to recruit people, and the right people.

Most churches continue to recruit informally, with nothing in writing, but there are drawbacks to this method. One is that, without listing what you need, you could be excluding those who feel they have limited skills to offer but would in fact be ideal. Or you may not attract someone with little experience who may, however, want to try something different if they knew a little more of what it involves.

It is worth thinking about developing role (or task) descriptions: short documents that you can give to people to help them see whether they are suitable for the role or not. These are like job descriptions in that they detail exactly what the role entails and show a prospective volunteer exactly to what they would be committing themselves. It will help them answer the questions, 'Am I the round peg they are looking for, or am I more suited to a square hole?' Be careful, however, that you do not use the word 'job' anywhere in a role description, as it can suggest it is a contract of employment, even if no payment is involved. Some volunteer organisations advise against having role descriptions at all for this reason, but I feel they have a place and, provided they are worded properly, can only be useful[67]—and not just for the volunteer.

Producing a role description can help you think exactly what you want from a volunteer. They can also help avoid misunderstandings: 'But, I thought I'd be helping with the under 5s...' as the volunteer is confronted with a lively group of nine-year-olds. Role descriptions do not have to be hugely detailed—three pages for a volunteer to make coffee after the service, for example, would be excessive and off-putting, but in that situation it would be really useful to include whether or not they need to provide the milk.

It is worth producing such a description for every volunteer position, no matter how large or small. Knowing the duties, expectations and responsibilities of both the volunteer and the organisation simplifies the recruitment, selection and management of volunteers. Developing such documents also encourages you to make the roles as interesting and rewarding as they can be. A detailed volunteer role description is particularly useful if you are recruiting through a volunteer agency or other third party. It saves time and disappointment on both sides if a potential volunteer knows as much as possible about the role before getting in touch.

It is also a good risk management approach. Good role descriptions allow everyone to know where they stand. They ameliorate risk and, if necessary, are documents you can refer to should anything go wrong. It is hardly fair to criticise or discipline a volunteer who has never been given a clear understanding of their role in the first place.

Volunteer agreements

Allied to role descriptions are volunteer agreements. These are documents that set out exactly what is expected of the volunteer in terms of adherence to policies and also what your organisation can offer them, in terms of support, training, supervision and out of pocket expenses.[68]

Some organisations combine the two documents into one

(there are many examples on the internet). I recommend that they are kept separate as the volunteer agreement is more of a policy document and longer term while the role description is much more specific and requires regular updating.

Probationary period

However good your role descriptions and volunteer agreements, you may find that someone offers with enthusiasm but is just not suited to the role. If you have an agreed probationary period in place, then you have an easy way, on both sides, to end a volunteer's time without embarrassment. Six months is a long enough period to see if someone really 'fits'. For a simpler activity three months may be adequate (although not for an event that happens only monthly). Probationary periods are also useful for those who may have the skills, but simply don't 'perform'. At the end of that time you should arrange a meeting to talk things through. (See Chapter 11 for more thoughts of how to have 'that conversation'.)

Supervision/appraisals

These are concepts from the corporate world now being seen in the area of volunteering. Having been involved in both areas, I can speak for their value. They can sound rather formal and off-putting, so you may want to use other language, such as mentoring and review. What is important is that there is a proper system in place. Obviously a volunteer can leave at any time but may not want to ask for a break when they really need one for fear of letting the group down. It is important to provide opportunities for this. A clear understanding that a role is not for life will make a surprising difference to how people feel, and quite likely to your ability to recruit. You will find that younger people actually expect this kind of procedure; that they will be disappointed otherwise and indeed may not come forward as volunteers at all.

In our Diocese (group of churches under a Bishop) both Readers (Lay worship leaders and preachers) and pastoral ministers have a three-year licence, with an opportunity to look at their formal working agreement before they are re-licensed. At my own church some people have either changed their role or asked to step back for a period on each of these occasions. Personally I like to have more frequent conversations than this, ideally annually, but at least the diocesan process is built in and ensure the review happens. This is something to work on with your volunteers—what would they like, and what is realistic for you to offer. There are no hard and fast rules, but best practice and my own experience suggest that more frequently, within reason, is better than less. It may stop resentment growing or enable issues to be resolved before a crisis point is reached. It can simply be a positive, affirming chat. Since relationships are so important the time spent with individuals is never wasted.

If nothing more, such a meeting is an annual reminder that the person is still valued, indeed still remembered! I was doing one on behalf of a neighbouring church. After we had talked for a while a rather wistful look came on the volunteer's face. She told me that she had never had a detailed conversation like that, to talk about what she did and how she felt about it, in all the years she had been there. She did meet regularly with her former minister, but only for 'what to do next' kind of conversations, never questions about her and what she needed. Regular appraisals, or more informal conversations if you prefer, are important, because people are not always good at articulating for themselves exactly how they feel.

Simply meeting for a chat will not necessarily be adequate. You might need to work quite hard to draw some things out, as people will not always venture opinions, even when you ask them. This might include:

- what they are really good at (they may tell you what they enjoy doing, but that is not the same thing)
- what they are tired of doing
- what they need, in terms of training and resources to be able to do their role better
- when they need a sabbatical

Sabbaticals

Sabbaticals are built in to most church ministers' pattern of work, yet I have never come across the phrase in relation to volunteers until recently. We all know volunteers who have done the same task for 30 years and love it, but a break is good for everyone.

At our church we do not have a paid organist or worship leader but rely on a number of volunteers. One of the most talented came to me saying that he wanted not only to step down from leading, but even from playing the music in church. He had been doing it for many years and simply needed a break, to worship. Another person, who regularly led worship and preached also asked for a break when she did not have enough time to give the tasks adequate preparation.

What you should try to avoid at all costs is having some people in your church who are simply too busy with church activities. They say 'yes' to requests because they feel an obligation or guilt, or just because there is no one else to take on a task. Tiring people out, even worse burning them out, is uncaring and pastorally poor practice. I cannot, hand on heart, say that I have *never* allowed anyone to get too busy, but I have tried very hard not to. As soon as I have been made aware of such a situation, I have tried to deal with it. I have an absolute rule that, when looking to start new ventures, we have an adequate team in place first. It is hard to do without an activity that seems expected in a church, but if you simply do not have the people to run it adequately it is better not to have it for a while than to burn people out. Burnout is dreadful for the person concerned, with all sorts of short and possibly long-term consequences for them as well as for the work. It can mean others will be reluctant to step forward if they know that this is how they are likely to be treated. It also reflects badly on the church as a whole, so is a poor witness to the loving and caring God we worship.

So, when you ask people how things are going, use all your senses to judge their response. We may miss the 'micro-expressions' we all use unconsciously, but drooping shoulders or hitting their head with their hand is easier to spot! Just as important, make it part of your job to look out for signs of burnout in the volunteers you already have. Does anyone seem to lack energy, enthusiasm, motivation? Do they no longer seem to be getting the same satisfaction out of their activity as they used to? Is their interest flagging? Perhaps their sense of humour is not as it was, or their planning, which used to be immaculate, becomes sloppy. Being able to pick up these warning signs means that you need to know your volunteers well, to have a genuine relationship, which involves spending time with them to see how they are really feeling, not just the usual British token conversation: 'How are things going?' 'Fine, thanks.' 'That's great; keep up the good work.'

We must also take into account people's personal circumstances. Is work particularly tough for them at the moment? Are they studying? Does their stage of family life mean that they need to spend more time at home, or ferrying the children around? Are there other pressures which mean some extra space would be good?

A young mum who had been very involved withdrew as her children reached school age. Other professionals and volunteers were pretty miffed at what seemed a drop in commitment, to both Sunday worship and midweek activities. Far from 'writing her off', I kept the communication channel open, so that she could return again once her children were older.

Sometimes you have to play a very long game—indeed such a long game that you, personally, might not be around to see that person come back and develop a whole new season of service. Pressurising someone, trying to keep them too much in your church or group is probably the most effective way of driving them away.

Exit interviews

These are now standard practice in the business world and professional charity sector, and should be in volunteering. It could be seen as the final debrief, but on a more personal level it is an opportunity to show how much you value their insights, that you want to hear how they feel and to have a chance to say 'thank you'.

Procedure for 'virtual' volunteers

You might expect that these are somehow easier or different to manage but all the same issues are there, albeit at a distance rather than face to face. And you will need to work hard at building a relationship with someone you rarely, or never, see.

Chapter 10

Saying 'thank you'

'Someone just saying thank you helps enormously. If no one ever says thank you, you feel as if no one really cares enough.' A lack of thanks can be disastrous. The right kind of thanks, given at the right time and in the right way, is absolutely crucial.

Our Deanery Standing Committee had a great idea. We wanted to affirm the many individuals in our churches who are working with young people, so we organised a tea party and planned a special service. The aim was to say a sincere 'thank you'. As part of the afternoon we had a workshop to discuss future ideas for young peoples' work but feedback after the event was quite negative. Volunteers felt they had been brought along under false pretences. We had thought involving them in forming the future would be affirming, but they wanted an afternoon which showed that what they were already doing was valued.

I remember an early conversation with a new member at my church. She and her husband had formerly been worshipping elsewhere, and slowly but surely, they had been asked to take on more and more. That was not the problem (I suspect they are doing more now than they were in their previous church). The problem, they told me, was that they were taken for granted. It was simply assumed they would take on the next thing when asked. I never make that assumption. You should never take the work your volunteers do for granted; it is their precious time they are giving.

Not everyone wants recognition; in fact some really do not.

(Others *say* they do not. You will soon learn which is which). The important point is that people know you are grateful for all they do, and sometimes for other people to know too.

'Don't thank me, thank God'

That is the response I was once advised to give if anyone said to me, 'Thanks for that sermon', but I think that is wrong. More than that, I think it is churlish, ungracious, and it throws the compliment back in someone's face. There is a 'super Christian' attitude that you should not need anyone to say 'thank you', which probably comes from a misunderstanding of such passages as Matthew 6:1: 'Don't do your good deeds publicly, to be admired by others, for you will lose the reward from your Father in heaven' (NLT). Some church leaders feel it is not their role to thank people, because God will reward them in due course. Yet that passage is about acts of charity and conspicuous prayer, not practical help. You can hardly avoid doing the latter in public—at the very least, those in the group you are helping will know.

I know we are doing everything for God, and that should be adequate reward but, hey, we are human and, being human, we like to be thanked. And what is wrong with that? Paul is often thought of as being very strict, always ready to criticise and correct, but he was free with praise too (see, for example 1 Corinthians 11:2; Romans 1:8; Ephesians 1:16). We need to know what people think of what we are doing and it is good to give and receive thanks. We are trained to give it from an early age because it is important.

People gain a lot of satisfaction from knowing they have 'done a good job', but how will they know without feedback? I think of one lady in our congregation who, some 40 or more years ago, was running a youth organisation. I frequently meet people locally who remember her with fondness, and whenever they pass a compliment to me, I pass it straight on. It is important to know that what you are giving of your life makes a difference, so all leaders should do all they can to make sure volunteers know.

Thank you for...

The 'W' questions—'what?', 'when?', 'why?', 'where' and 'how?' (and, of course, 'who?')—are really useful here.

Why should we thank people?

Because it is good for us, for them and for the Body as a whole. The Bible is full of injunctions to praise (give thanks to) God. If God thinks praise is a good thing and we are made in his image, does it not make sense that we need both to give and to get praise too? Some people object to the notion of praising, even of praising God. A scene in the Peter Cook and Dudley Moore film *Bedazzled* has Cook, as the Devil, getting Moore to circle him on a post box saying, 'Oh, how great you are, how wonderful.' Not surprisingly, Moore soon gets bored. I hope our vision of heaven, and the reasons we praise God, are broader than that.

What is Romans chapter 16 except a long list of people Paul wanted to thank? 'She has been the benefactor..., are grateful to them..., worked very hard for you... They are outstanding... whose fidelity to Christ has stood the test... who work hard ..., who has worked very hard..., who has been a mother to me.' Paul often thanked God *for* people, as I hope we do, but he also clearly thanked people as well.

The Gospels do not record the times Jesus said 'thank you', but I get the impression this was part of his way. I interpret that Jesus was being free with praise when he said to the 72 who had just returned to him, 'I saw Satan fall like lightning from heaven' (Luke 10:18). He knew the disciples had done a good job, and he let them know what he thought.

What are you thanking them for?

Be as specific as you can. There is a place for the general 'thanks for everything you have done this week'. As I sat down to write this, I had just returned from taking part in our older people's holiday club (run entirely by volunteers) where I was asked to give a vote of general thanks to all the helpers. That is often the way in public praise (which I will come back to). For personal praise, however precisely you give it, be as specific as possible: 'Thank you for that wonderful flower arrangement', '... for the excellent music in the service today', '... for clearing up the mess when that child was sick in the pew'.

When should you thank people?

The simplest answer could be as often as possible. Providing you are following the advice for 'what', you will not get into that contemporary trend of over-praising a child for every small, ordinary thing they do, so they come to expect it and may no longer strive to excel.

Generally 'when' should be as close as possible to the time of the action, or as soon as you can afterwards. To take the last example above: you should thank the person for clearing up a mess at the time, not some weeks later, when they are likely to have forgotten all about it. There are occasions, such as the Annual General Meeting, when you can offer general thanks to large numbers of people for work over a long time period, but that must not be the only time you thank them. If I had not, at some point in the previous year, given personal thanks to every single person I was globally thanking at such a meeting, I would be very disappointed with myself.

A clergyman was giving his report at the church's AGM one year. He had spent a lot of time preparing his list of whom to thank for what but one lady was missed out. She immediately resigned.

That sort of situation is my nightmare. I spend more time anguishing over this element than over almost anything else for such meetings. Not everyone will react like that lady, but just think how you yourself feel when you have, or have not, been thanked for a task after you have put a lot of work into it. It is not that most of us want the credit. Indeed we may well feel embarrassed when our name is mentioned. Yet if our name is not mentioned, might there not be just a flutter of 'why not'?

Where do you thank them?

Both in private and in public. In private most often and in public when it seems right. You can offer a quiet word or email immediately after the event, a more public mention at the next meeting or service, a special mention on an 'occasion' for something really important.

How do you thank them?

There are so many ways. Here are a few suggestions to start you thinking:

- Direct personal thanks. Take time to talk and express your appreciation. Remind them of their value to the team, to the church, and to God.
- Pray for them at church. This will show that the church is taking not just them but their area of work seriously. All too often some aspects of church work, especially with young people, goes on with little contact with the wider congregation.
- Mention them at a group meeting.
- Commission new people publically.
- Focus regularly on different groups and individual volunteers in your church magazine. Also tell their stories in the local paper. This is encouraging for them and good for the reputation of your church.
- Create a photo collage or slide show of volunteer activities for display.
- Publicise any external recognition they gain. When our bell-ringers win a trophy, it is displayed in church for a few weeks.

- Having a 'thank you' party.
- Take the team out for a meal/burger.
- Have a 'fun' event, for example, bowls evening/cinema/paintball/ museum. You will know what works for your team. If not, ask.
- Arrange an 'awards ceremony', perhaps on a community basis, not just your church.
- Nominate volunteers for local or national awards.
- Acknowledge the work done at the AGM, possibly along with publishing a list of all the people who volunteer across your church/organisation.
- Send birthday cards.
- Give small gifts, for example, a bunch of flowers, chocolates, a bottle of wine, vouchers. Find something a bit special, to make them feel a bit special.
- 'Thank you' notes/email. Which is best depends on the person, and may be age specific—older people will appreciate a handwritten card, others are happy with email, others with face-to-face conversations.
- Pass on positive comments you hear. Do not keep praise to yourself. When someone commented to me that 'that was the best Baptism service I have ever been to', I immediately passed that on to the music leader, baptism visitors and welcomers—all those who were involved.
- A phone call for no other reason than to say 'thank you', and make it a little longer conversation to see how they are getting on. I wonder whether ministers do not want to talk to people for long in case they really do open up and share a problem!
- Ask their advice. This is a way of showing how much you value what they are doing.
- Invite them for coffee or lunch.
- Give 'goodies'—pens, USB sticks, baseball caps, fluffy bugs (best for younger volunteers)[69]
- Recognise anniversaries with your organisation. When our 'tower captain', the person who organises the bell-ringing, passed 50

years in the role he was presented with a special certificate in the service, and an article in the church magazine. That might not seem a lot, but it made a difference.

- Mark 'retirements' adequately, and also if someone moves on from your church.
- Sponsor their attendance at training activities, workshops, seminars. Training is a strong factor in retention too. It is not just that volunteers will feel valued if you support or organise training, but that they will become even more enthusiastic as they learn more. One group I work with runs a conference every couple of years to bring the scattered groups of volunteers together, as a way of saying thank you and to make sure they keep 'on message'. It is a residential conference, so the budget for this is not inconsiderable, but it is a fraction of what we would have to pay if we relied on professionals to do what the volunteers do. It is thus an excellent investment.
- Give them additional responsibilities. Yes, this can be encouraging, as they realise their gifts and time are valued.

Planning your thanks

Thanking people properly needs not just the emotional intelligence to be aware of when you need to say thanks. It takes careful planning. I love to encourage people, but I have two problems—a bad memory and a chaotic time management system. I sometimes miss opportunities and that is where email comes in handy. Yes, I know, it is not as personal as a face-to-face conversation, but it can be filed away by the recipient in a way that a personal comment cannot. Above all, make sure you have a system of noting down who needs to be thanked, and then applying the questions above.

For a number of years I have given small gifts at Christmas to those who have an 'official' position within the church. I have thought quite carefully about who should receive one, and whether those who do not might feel in some way left out. (As it happens, I have not picked up any such feeling.) Wherever possible I have tried to visit personally to hand out the gifts. This has proved difficult in some years, but I plan to persevere. I know one volunteer team leader who is brilliant at giving absolutely everyone involved in her projects a 'thank you' card at the end, including the minister! In another church an anonymous donor supplies all the holiday club volunteers with a bar of chocolate. Paul writes in more than one letter that he always gives thanks (see, for example, Philippians 1:3). Be creative in the ways you do this.

A gift that costs nothing...

Some of these ideas cost nothing, others will cost a reasonable amount. Be careful, as this can be a sensitive subject. As Communication Director for CMS I spent time with local groups of volunteers around the country, to find out what their concerns were, how we might help and resource them, and to thank them, in person. This last item was not always easy. I vividly remember visiting a small support group at a local café. The ladies were horrified (that is not putting it too strongly) when I offered to pay for their tea and a bun. I did it as a small gesture of thanks, but they wanted every penny of the money they raised to go to mission, which I completely understood. I thus learnt to be slightly more subtle, and to find other ways of saying thank you! If you are concerned about costs and have a limited budget, consider approaching an appropriate local or national company for sponsorship.

Once I was involved with a proper 'prize giving' style event. We organised some decent snacks and drinks, invited the bishop and made a social event out of it. Along with the presentation of certificates there was an opportunity for people to say what the course had meant to them. This took a fair bit of organisation. From the responses we received afterwards, and for the long-term benefits this brought, the effort was very much worthwhile— that in itself a boost to those who organised the event. The original idea was for something simpler, just coffee and biscuits, but I doubt that would have worked anything like as well. After all, coffee and biscuits happens in most churches at most meetings, and we wanted to make this evening a bit special. How much should you spend? This topic might make an interesting discussion at your church council: 'We have a budget for the various elements of our work. Should we build in an element for saying thank you?'

Valuing their time

What is important and costs absolutely nothing is not wasting a volunteer's time. This is part of treating them with respect. You do this by, for example, only calling meetings when you need them, and being properly prepared when you do. Although there are some who love the minutiae of committee life, this is *not* a need a church should be seeking to meet. Think about when you may need to have to meet physically or when you might use an email discussion or even a phone conference instead. These might be a better way of spending everyone's time.

I talked in Chapter 6 about the 'adjourning' stage of team formation. One way of saving valuable time is to see if you can set up working groups rather than committees for anything with a specific focus. Once that task is over, the group naturally comes to an end. This can help in recruiting too. Men in particular prefer to know just what they are letting themselves in for when they 'sign up' and are more likely to join something called a working party than a committee. Committees can develop a life of their own, and have a habit of absorbing large amounts of time. Keep your committees to a minimum, and keep those you have efficient— and spread them out a bit further. Whenever I have joined an organisation, I have increased the time between various meetings.

Rarely have I found that people miss them or that the work does not get done.

A group of five people were planning a service. It was nearly finished and ready to be handed over to the minister. The minister's wife said that he was too busy to finish it off, so insisted that people stayed until it was completed. Rather than it taking the minister around an hour to complete, it involved nearly an hour of five people's time. The minister's time was seen as that much more valuable.

If you are a leader, be prepared to spend your own time on those you lead. Be available to them. If I was to point to the most important truth I have discovered in leading volunteers, I would say this was it, especially important if they have problems or simply need to know something. On the day I was writing this section, I had two people needing some of my time, one immediately, one involving me in both an immediate reply and further work. I had to respond, although both requests were cutting into time I had allocated to something else. People may need time to talk, to think through ideas, even simply to feel acknowledged. To say, 'Sorry, I'm too busy to talk right now'—or simply to ignore a request— suggests to your volunteers that your time is more valuable than theirs.

It's a really good idea to work out the amount of time people put in for the benefit of your organisation or church, then work out how much time you give them. I would expect to see a significant multiplying factor. You can then do a calculation as to the value of that time. This would be an informative paragraph to add somewhere in your annual report. You might just find that this gives you even more incentive to say 'thank you'.

Chapter 11

Problems, conflict and ending well

Within Christian circles there is often an expectation that everything should be 'nice', that all relationships will be perfect, since we are brothers and sisters in Christ. Those of us who work for Christian organisations know otherwise, know that sin is as much within the Body of Christ as without. We are working in a fallen world and need God's grace in all we do. We follow a Lord who calls his disciples to 'take up their cross' (Matthew 16:24) in order to follow him—and for leaders, a small part of carrying that cross are those tough decisions you have to make. Paul had to deal with a whole range of problems: wrong thinking, wrong behaviour, direct conflict and more. The best known example is possibly when Peter had stopped eating with Gentile Christians because of pressures from other Christians, as Paul puts it: 'When Cephas came to Antioch, I opposed him to his face' (Galatians 2:11).

Most of us will have had times when we have to deal with problems, criticism and conflict between volunteers or between paid staff and volunteers, volunteers who do not do what they should, or simply volunteers who have done a really good job but are now past their 'best before' date. What Bible guidelines might help us in dealing with these sorts of issues?

The passage to start with is Matthew 18:15–17: 'If a fellow believer hurts you, go and tell him...' (*THE MESSAGE*). There is no detail about the specific issue (most translations use 'sin') in this passage, but the 'fault' is clearly something serious. From this I understand the importance of:

- going to the person directly first, and as soon as possible. They may not even be aware that they are doing something wrong, or have hurt you or others in some way. Make them aware of the problem (as accurately and dispassionately as possible). All being well, you can resolve the issue and agree a way forward without the situation deteriorating. But, if not…
- go with one or two others. Take other members of the team with you, people that you both know. Not only will there be no risk of either party starting false rumours (which sadly does happen) but the others may be able to act as witnesses to the problem itself and point out its seriousness. Again the hope is that the matter is dealt with. But, if not…
- bring it to the attention of the wider church. I would suggest this is through the leadership, eldership, whatever your normal channels are. It is important that it does not stay with a single leader. If she has to act, then at the very least make a report to whatever wider accountability group you have, again as soon as possible. By the time you have reached this stage there may already be several others involved.

In the secular world this would be described as 'escalation'. The principles are actually very similar, but we have the elements of prayer and forgiveness to offer. Christian leaders must constantly offer forgiveness and reconciliation, the opportunity for a new start, because people learn by making mistakes as well as by developing new skills. I interpret Jesus' reaction to the disciples' failure in Luke 9:41 as having a hint of frustration about it, but he both sorted the problem out and explained why they had failed, so that next time they could do better.

The story in Acts 15 tells of a problem wider than one between individuals; it affected whole churches. Paul and Barnabas had obviously not been able to get a resolution locally, so they returned to 'head office'. Here the case was heard clearly, the leaders thought long and hard about it, prayed, and a decision on the way forward was reached. Whatever the scale of the problem, seek God's will for a resolution. Be as objective as you can (do not let your feelings and personal likes and dislikes get the better of you). Ensure you keep respect for the individual at the front of your mind. Do not talk down to them, and try to be as understanding as possible, keeping the problem in perspective.

The 'flip' side of this is Matthew 5:23–24: 'If you… remember that your brother or sister has something against you.' You cannot worship God properly if you have unresolved issues with others. That is why many churches have introduced 'the peace' into services, to give people a liturgical opportunity to clear the air. It is far better, though, if you can resolve a situation beforehand or begin the process then and continue it later.

Conflict

One of the worst medical problems is what is called an 'auto-immune' disease, where the immune system mistakes some part of the body as a pathogen, an enemy, and attacks its own cells. It leads to a literal breaking down of the body. Conflict is an 'auto-immune' problem for the Body of Christ: 'If you bite and devour each other, watch out or you will be destroyed by each other' (Galatians 5:15).

I am not someone who welcomes conflict, who feels that 'a good argument' clears the air. I find it stressful; I find it painful. I would much rather it did not happen, because sometimes it affects relationships that I value. Yet I have learnt that conflict has to be faced and worked through, or matters will simply get worse. I would say my position is 'conflict averse' but not 'conflict avoidant'. Think about your own approach to conflict: are you 'avoidant'? Or perhaps you take one of these other classic positions?

- Accommodative: likely to go for appeasement (backing down) or satisfying the other's needs while forgoing your own
- Competitive: a desire to win; not concerned for the other
- Compromising: sharing outcomes, 'splitting the difference'
- Collaborative: tries to aim for a win–win; cooperative, with both sides gaining something

Make an honest assessment. If you take any of the first three, then I suggest you talk to someone about why, and work on changing it. 'Compromising' sounds a bit better that the other options initially, and sometimes it could be a way out. But there are some issues over which you cannot compromise. The final one, collaborative, is the one to aim for, because it involves both parties treating each other with respect and using reason. I would say that it is the only truly Christian approach.

You may have to deal with conflict between or among volunteers. For example, you may have two excellent volunteers who just cannot get on with one another. You may have to move one of them out of the team—which one is a matter for careful thought

Mind your language

A key part of resolving such issues is 'active listening'. Active listening helps you to hear the emotion and affirm the person. You listen to understand what a person is saying, feeling or thinking and then put your understanding into words and feed it back to them. You do not express your own feelings or come up with solutions. This communicates that 'I hear what you are feeling', 'I understand how you see things', 'I am interested and concerned about you' (as well as about the situation and the other volunteers).[70]

Think very carefully about the language you use in such con-versations. Avoid 'you' statements, such as 'you aren't making any sense', and replace them with 'I' statements, such as 'I couldn't understand what you said'. Try to keep things factual—'on three occasions you have…' rather than 'you often…' (even worse, 'you always…'). Use descriptive language; explain why their behaviour is a problem (they genuinely might not have realised). Be clear about what you want to see in terms of action—a change in behaviour, going on some training or stopping taking part in an activity? Do all you can to make any criticism constructive.

You may not just be dealing with a particular individual, of course. Sometimes you may be mediating when conflict breaks out among two or more people. You can use the same skills to mediate or get the parties involved to talk in problem-solving language. First use active listening with both sides to calm their emotions. Then use open questions (who? what? when? where? how?) such as 'What do you see happening?', 'How are you feeling about…?', 'What has X done/not done that bothers you?', 'What do you think we could do?' Encourage people to be specific; do not allow generalities. Ask questions about the emotions involved: 'How do you feel about that?' Try to get each to see the other side, remaining neutral if you can (and assuming the specific resolution does not matter). Then, to conclude, you can ask a question or series of questions, such as, 'What do you want X to do or not do instead?'

You may need to talk to other volunteers as part of this process but make sure you are very circumspect. Never comment on one volunteer to another in a negative way. Praise, on the other hand, is never harmful.

Performance issues

At a level beneath actual conflict there is another area that is often avoided but that will equally result in negative outcomes: when a person is not performing very well. Perhaps they used to be fine, but the role has developed beyond their capabilities. Perhaps the person has a talent, but they are in the wrong role and need moving, or the role is too tough for them. If so, then, for their sake as well as that of the work, you need to move them on. Offer them the chance to do less but not to withdraw altogether. You might find that this is exactly what they want, and they have not had the courage to discuss it with you. See if providing extra support or training will help them, or look at other ways of equipping them. In the end, if that is not possible, you have to ask them to move.

Thus comes the point where you have to have 'that conversation'. How could you do that?

- Begin by asking them how they are getting on, to pick up any issue you may then need to work on.
- Express appreciation for all that they have been doing.
- Be specific on the issues, and keep checking them out with the person to see if they have noticed anything themselves. Do not be negative, carping or overly critical. Be factual and firm. If they trust your judgment in other areas, they may begin to see how it bears on their own situation.
- While you are in the conversation, keep assessing how important it is that you resolve the situation there and then. Could you give them a few more weeks or months to see if things change? If the person can improve and they are simply struggling in one or two areas, a way forward might involve to avoid those areas.
- Talk about what else they may wish to do instead. As with an appraisal, it is not good to go into a discussion with no constructive ways out. Ideally go armed with a few alternatives that you think might appeal to them.
- Offer training if you can, or ask them to explore what may be available. Again, the better prepared you are before the conversation, the easier it will be. If you have nothing to offer, it can end up a very negative experience.
- Be firm in your resolve. Do not allow the conversation to go in directions that mean you never actually get round to making the points you intended (and yes, I know, I have done that too).

- End the time on a positive note, talking of their strengths and gifts, offering your help and support in helping them move forward and look forward to what they can continue to offer rather than only what they can no longer do.
- Again express appreciation for all that they have been doing.

Clear expectations are important. It is hardly fair if problems arise because a person has or has not done something because they did not know about it. Equally, a potential problem could be avoided if you and/or the volunteer can be a bit more flexible about certain things, if your project can work with this. And get feedback from other volunteers about how reasonable they think you are being.

In the last chapter I raised the idea of having a proper disciplinary policy. To have such a policy shows that you take this matter seriously. Even if you do not, there is much we can learn from such an approach, which ensures that the rights of the individual as well as the organisation are respected. We can give proper warnings, keep careful records so that we have good documented evidence, offer opportunities for correction, give a limited timeframe for delivery of results, and such like. If serious issues do arise, you may want to take advice from others outside your immediate group.

An issue might be temporary. Perhaps someone has had a bereavement or is going through a tough time at work. They may feel really bad about letting the team down, yet they are not functioning properly, so it is doing neither them nor the work any good. It is important to help them to see that and perhaps to realise that a short break may be better for everyone in the long run, even if that means that some work might not get done or be done less well. Interestingly, though, for some people tough times can be a spur to further work, as it helps them get through by expending time, energy and emotion on others. It gives them a safe space where they can put their own problems to one side.

Then there are some people who are just difficult to place: 'She gave her life for others. You could tell the others by the haunted look on their faces.'[71] Some people love to be wanted. They may even have considerable skills to offer but end up causing problems wherever they are. Can you find this person a role that does not involve them working alongside others, perhaps something more administrative or in preparation? If that person really wants to be with others, you may be able to put them with a particularly skilled team leader. But there may come a time when you have to say 'no'.

Is getting old a problem?

Dealing with people whose age is causing difficulty is perhaps the hardest; they may have been faithfully doing a job for years but are simply no longer capable. Some find it very hard to let go. They cling on because their value is tied up with what they do for the church. For them to stop means they feel 'useless', 'discarded', that they are just 'pew fodder'. (These are all words used to me by others. I cannot stress too strongly that they should never be used by anyone responsible for others).

How often do we hear something like, 'I know her flower arrangements look like she has just thrown them in, but it gives her a lot of pleasure', or 'Yes, I know, we have to go around the lawn a second time after he's cut it, but how will he feel if we ask him to stop?'

It's great when people realise the situation for themselves. I can think of at least two individuals who helped me in this. One instance happened soon after I moved to a new church. Somebody who I knew had been a leader in another church would faithfully come each Sunday, and I felt bad that he was never asked to take part in some way. One day I asked him if he would lead the prayers. 'No,' he said, 'I've had my time; it's for others to take this on now.' That was a very honest assessment. A woman whose gifts in prayer and Bible study I valued greatly got to the point where she was reluctant to take part in public worship. I thought she was still quite capable, but she was worried that others would think she was not. So, with some reluctance, I took her off the rota a year or two earlier than I might otherwise have done. Having said this, there are others who, even when you have a conversation with them, or drop quite heavy hints, just don't seem to pick up on the reality of the situation.

A straightforward issue is that of volunteer drivers. Whatever your skills in this area, they tend to decline with age. A point comes where the safety of those driven outweighs consideration for the feelings of the volunteer. There may also be issues over insurance. Most organisations have a policy which involves a definite age cut-off point for drivers, so there is a natural and expected (although not always happily accepted) resolution. Some individuals may well still be quite capable. You can commiserate with them, but you still have to follow the rules.

The Church of England has a system whereby no one can retain a licensed ministry (being officially accredited within a church) beyond the age of 70. However, they can have special permission to continue if they are able. That is helpful as it allows those who can do so to continue (and I have several over 70s, and even in a couple of instances over 80s who remain valued members of the team in regular ministry). There is also the title of 'emeritus', which is given to some, and also allows a certain 'honorary' role for those who have served faithfully over the years. At the same time, we must help people realise that retirement is an honourable option.

Organists constitute another area. So far the Church of England at least has no age policy with regard to them. There may be no danger to life and health, but since worship is such a central activity for a church, the organist's competence is still a major issue. I have had to deal with exactly this in the past, with an organist who began to play more and more wrong notes. I tried to apply the principles I have just outlined:

1. I did not jump in as soon as the first wrong note was played. I monitored the situation for a few months to see if this was a consistent issue. It was.
2. I talked with the person responsible for the coordination of musicians and had X removed from main services, retaining them for occasional ones, about which they were happy enough.
3. When it became clear that the problem was getting worse (albeit affecting fewer people), I felt I needed to take things further.
4. I spoke to someone I trusted who is very sensitive pastorally. She was actually relieved, as she herself had a growing concern. I spoke to someone else, who knew both the person and situation, for further advice.
5. I rang X and arranged to go round for a chat, to talk through what their commitment might be. I asked about how things were, and how they felt, trying, subtly, to suggest a lesser commitment might be a good idea. It became clear they had no awareness that there was a problem at all. I left, somewhat disheartened at my lack of communication skills.
6. I shared my findings with those I had talked to earlier and we agreed to work towards that person's 'retirement' through a progressive reduction in their appearing on the rota and through involving other musicians more often.

Had I dealt adequately with the situation? No. I had been steeling myself for another, more direct, conversation but as it turned out, within a few weeks a health issue meant that X could not continue in that position. What if that had not been the case? Could I have allowed this to continue? No, I could not. It would not have been fair on the congregation, nor on X, because of the grumbling that would have undoubtedly grown. In this particular case I would even have been prepared to move to a system of recorded music if no other musicians could have been found. If you are in a similar situation, ask yourself if that is another way forward.

Problems that people do not think they have

The previous couple of sections have looked at dealing with problems of individuals who are no longer performing. There are other occasions where you have to act simply because knowledge or legislation has changed. This does not always make matters easier.

We have some ancient church silver. A few years ago advice about how to care for it changed. No longer were creams and lotions, even specially formulated ones, to be used, but only a quick rinse given after use. Like many churches, we had a faithful team of ladies who did such cleaning. We prepared the ground carefully, explaining why the procedure needed to change.[72] We thanked them for what they had been doing, speaking personally to every member of the team. They still felt bereft and that somehow they were being accused of having done things wrong. The procedures matter, though. I have learnt since that, many years before, the group were known to be using a well-known brass cleaner to clean a silver-plated chalice. No one tackled the problem, which means there is now very little silver left on it!

Act swiftly

Whatever the issue, it is important to act as soon as possible after it has been brought to your attention. I have known church leaders who have avoided dealing with difficult problems, especially conflict, or difficult people, at all costs and, sadly, the costs have been considerable—always to the church, and often to them too. Ignoring an issue, tiptoeing around it, is not healthy. Focused prayer and careful thought are important before you get involved in any action, but do not let that become an excuse for not acting.

I have a friend whose favourite psalm is Psalm 133, which begins 'How good and pleasant it is when God's people live together in unity!' Nothing destroys that unity quicker than a problem that is not dealt with. Conflict does not have to destroy that unity; differences of opinion do not have to destroy that unity. Energies can be channelled and the church can move forward. Handled badly, these issues are negative and destructive. They affect our witness, waste precious time and resources and destroy relationships. They lead to poor morale, pessimism, division, despair. Delaying dealing with them only makes it all worse.

To allow known problems to continue is neither good leadership nor pastorally responsible. If there is a problem, then you must deal with it, for the sake of all those concerned. I have known ministers who go to a church where there is a 'problem person'; when the minister leaves, years later, that person is still in place. If you cannot bring yourself to have a conversation at any other time, at least do it in your last few months in post so there is one fewer issue for your successor to resolve!

I have encouraged some people to rethink their position, or perhaps to move to some other role within the church more suited to their gifts and temperament. Sometimes I (although never alone and always with the support of others in leadership) have simply acted and sidelined that person. Pastoral care is one thing, and a crucially important one at that, but allowing one person, or a small group, to prevent action that you and others believe is God's purpose is quite another.

Begin much further back

I want to emphasise the crucial importance of a good relationship and the return on your investment of time in developing these. You should do all you can to build relationships with your volunteers so that, when a problem arises, you already have a foundation on which to build. If you have good, respectful, loving and trustful relationships within your church, then you have a much better chance of success when you may have to discipline a volunteer or ask them to change something they really like doing.

This is where regular meetings or just conversations about how things are going are useful. By asking people specific questions, they might then be able to articulate something they have not realised before and you might be surprised when they respond, 'Actually, I'm struggling at the moment, I'm wondering if I might have a break.' Think of Jesus and Peter in John 21:15–21. It may have been Jesus who is posing the question, 'Do you love me?', but it is also Jesus who shows most love. There are times when, however good the relationship, however much care you take to prepare and whatever you say, people will end up taking umbrage, even deciding they want to be hurt. You cannot prevent this; it is part of the pain of leadership.

There are some more general, low-level issues I want to address before finishing this chapter. A couple of modern 'folklore' characters provide other areas you may have to tackle among your volunteers.

Dealing with Private Fraser

You may remember—as I do—and smile at the *Dad's Army* character who was forever saying, 'We're all doomed, doomed!' Living with one is not so easy, but all churches have them: the doom-mongers, the naysayers, although I hope not too many of them. The kind of people who say:

'We'll never manage that.'

'But we've always done it this way.' (These are known as the 'seven last words of a dying church'.)

'The young people just aren't interested.'

'No one will take on that job.'

... and the Dementors

There are people who go way beyond Private Fraser. If you have read the 'Harry Potter' books, you will know about the Dementors ,who feed off human happiness, bringing depression and despair to anyone near them. There is a well-known joke in Church of England circles. A bishop is visiting a church with a long-serving churchwarden. 'You must have seen a lot of changes,' the bishop says, to make conversation. 'Aye,' the churchwarden replies, 'and I've opposed every one.' We may smile, but we should not forget that Dementors can also consume a person's soul, leaving them permanently dispirited and aimless.

How do you deal with them? A few suggestions:

1. Be positive. When I was doing a placement with a hospital chaplain, we were given an 'A–Z' for visiting patients. I have forgotten most of them, but 'W' has stuck in my mind: 'be well'. When the patients are giving their list of woes and ailments, do not try and outdo them with your own problems. Be empathetic, we were told. Listen, express concern, but do not give them anything to reinforce their own difficulties or to focus on yours. That is good advice for those in any level of church leadership. While being critical of the negative people in their own congregations, ministers will often be equally negative about 'them in head office'. Set an example and do not be drawn into the downward spiral of negativity. It is *not* about being a 'Pollyanna', relentlessly positive even in the face of evidence to the contrary. It *is* about not being unduly negative.

2. Offer alternative viewpoints. As a church leader you are likely to have a wider experience of church than most of your congregation. While nothing gets people down more quickly than the repeated use of the phrase, 'In my last church we did it like this...', you should be able to offer evidence of other ways that have worked, other ways of looking at the same

issue, stories where success has been achieved.

Think laterally. I am a great fan of the work of the scientist and author Edward de Bono who is generally credited with inventing lateral thinking and teaching thinking as a skill. He has described lateral thinking as the image of digging lots of holes until you hit the treasure rather than just continuing to dig one hole more and more deeply. He has also developed the 'Six Thinking Hats' process.[73] This is in some ways a freer version of the classic SWOT Analysis (Strengths, Weaknesses, Opportunities and Threats). Whichever you use, the important thing is to find a way of identifying alternatives that work for your group.

3. Provide some 'easy wins' to build up people's confidence. In the business world this is also known as 'low-hanging fruit'. Start with what you can do and work up from there. This will provide you with evidence to offer that proves that you can do something, even if not everything.

In our local community we wanted to improve the look of the shopping area at its centre, which consisted of some dreary 1960s buildings in need of a major make-over. There were issues over parking and litter-strewn areas. We decided that we would start by replanting the centre of a small roundabout that was presently just packed earth and rubbish. Red, white and blue flowers suddenly appeared (courtesy of a lot of hard work by a dedicated group of volunteers) and local people noticed. Alongside this we began to talk to the shop owners, local Councillors and others about ideas for developing the area. There is much more still to be done, but we have made a start.

If none of the above work, then you need to move up to the next level. People who are consistently negative and critical should be confronted rather than tolerated. Perhaps you have someone whose view is not just that the glass is half empty, but that it is cracked and needs throwing away and that no glass will actually ever be good enough. To help that person you ave to explore with them where the problem areas are. This is a place for truly honest conversations, but it is also the place for rapid and decisive action. A very difficult person can be demoralising to other team members and so cause them to leave ('I really don't need this at the end of a busy day'), perhaps with resentment at the church leadership for not having acted. Surely that is the worst of all possible worlds.

I have twice had people come to my church and volunteer to help, saying that God has sent them to deal with a particular sin or problem that they claimed was prevalent. I will never forget the look on the face of one of them when, after listening carefully to what they had to say, I told them I did not see any evidence of such a sin myself. That person left and never returned. I cannot remember how the other one reacted when I offered to do some asking around and get back to them; but they did not stay long. For the good of the church and the wider group you must deal with such things firmly, and as soon as you can.

Getting it wrong—the place for forgiveness

With all these areas it is essential to do everything you can to get the facts and process right. It is equally important that we are open when we get it wrong—and we *will* get it wrong. Those of us who lead must be prepared not just to offer forgiveness when someone lets us down but to seek forgiveness for our own failings.

Any leader can mess up and can end up demotivating people quite accidentally. We need to learn from our mistakes and oversights. We also need to forgive ourselves as well as ask forgiveness from those we have hurt. Loving others as we love ourselves (Mark 12:31) means exactly that.

The support of the Body

The support of others is very important when we get things wrong and even when we get it right. Sadly, even your best, most prayerful and diplomatic attempts at solving issues can come to nothing. People will still, almost wilfully, believe there are ulterior motives, no matter how often you say otherwise. They may still feel persecuted; they may be unhappy; they may develop a personal dislike of you. That is sad and difficult to cope with because no one likes to be thought of badly, and few cause pain to another willingly. For the sake of the greater good of the Body of Christ—the church—it is still important to act. It is still important to move the situation, or the person, on.

Remember: you are not alone when you have to make those decisions. Being part of the Body means there are others to help. If confidentiality is an issue, it may not be appropriate to talk to another volunteer but there is always the Senior Minister (and if you are that minister, there will be your church hierarchy or trusted Christian friends).

Chapter 12

Beyond the church walls

Although all the good practice I have encouraged in this book would work in secular as well as Christian circles, Christian volunteers have one crucial difference. They are working for the kingdom of God. Significantly, too (as I mentioned right at the beginning of this book), they do not only volunteer for church activities. There are churches I know, however, that keep a very close eye on their members and get worried if someone gives up a job within the church in order to take on another task in the wider community. Some think this means that the volunteer has 'left the work'.

Building people up as volunteers, providing support for them in whatever capacity they wish to volunteer, is not just for the benefit of the church, or even for those they serve in church. It is not even just for their own development as Christians. It is about building up the kingdom, enabling the Body to reach out into all walks of society, all professions, all social networks. It's about giving people skills and experiences that make them better people *for God* and for his mission. I am actually somewhat reluctant to ask members of the congregation to do jobs in church, because I want them to have time and energy to be witnesses in their other roles in life.

I want to encourage you not to be afraid of letting your volunteers 'escape' outside the church walls. It may indeed mean they have less time to devote to church projects, but they will be better for it. They will be using their God-given gifts in the widest arena possible. Crucially, they will be witnessing to the God they believe in to those alongside whom they are volunteering. Sometimes we as church leaders can be too precious, wanting to keep the best for ourselves. That was never Jesus' way.

Ann Morisy, in her book *Journeying Out*, talks about 'community chaplains' who '[help] people to sense the possibility of God' and 'rehabilitating the Church in people's minds'.[74] If we are going to witness to our wider community, we need to get beyond the church walls, and our volunteers are a significant way of doing this. We should not simply be sending out those with the gift of evangelism (which few in our churches feel they have in any case), but rather sending out people with each and every gift into each and every area of our community. In doing so, others will be able to see who we truly are, the love that drives us, and the God we believe in. It is also the way that we will become part of people's stories ('The potency of stories is that they transform inert facts into flesh-and-blood remembrances'),[75] and in so doing we can open up a way for others to become part of God's story. God will become real to them through the actions of his Body, you and me.

One of our congregation went through a three-year training course and was licensed as a pastoral worker. Her ministry was expressed predominantly through working as a counsellor with Relate. That was her official ministry, as listed on her working agreement. Her work was outside the church, and she was restricted in how much overt Christian input she could provide, but her faith was present in all she did. She was counted as being on the church volunteer team, and prayed for regularly. She was functioning as a part of the Body of Christ in the world. Another lady does not appear to be much involved in church activites. Yet she is often the first to tell me when someone needs help, or to arrive on someone's doorstep—sometimes mine—with some delicious home-made soup. That is not any kind of formal volunteering. She is never going to be 'signed up' with a role description and a 'Thank you for volunteering' bookmark, but she is a very active part of the Body, giving considerable time to others, and doing work for the kingdom.

The ministry of Street Angels[76] and Street Pastors[77] to the 'night-time economy' is a really interesting case in point. It is avowedly Christian and yet all about helping and serving some of those least likely to be in church on a Sunday morning. Encouraging congregation members to be involved in such activities might well prevent them doing other tasks in the church, although that is not my experience. Those involved in this kind of ministry from my church are also some of my busiest and most committed volunteers within church-based groups. I stand amazed and grateful to God for all they give.

This book has focused on 'building up the Body', the local church, in terms of strength, stamina, commitment, effectiveness and such like. That is body-building in the commonly understood sense. I also believe in 'building up the Body' in terms of size, in other words, numbers. When I was a radio broadcaster, I was called upon to speak to various groups of clergy and lay leaders. I talked about my own 'listening figures' and how, by working together, we might increase the numbers attending our churches. More than once I was met with the hostile response that 'church is not about numbers'. I agree that church is not *just* about numbers, that faithfulness and quality too are vital. Yet what is the Great Commission (Matthew 28:16–20) about if it is not about both? We are called to make disciples (quality) and to baptise people (quantity), and the recruiting, training, encouraging and deployment of our church members is key to both. The way we develop and use our volunteers is vital to the cause of mission, in providing the elements to build God's kingdom.

The current climate is more sympathetic to church-sponsored community work than it used to be. National and local government now welcome involvement of faith groups in wider society much more than was the case some years ago.[78] Although they talk in terms of 'community cohesion' or 'capacity building', there is a positive attitude to what faith groups can offer:

There is something special that makes faith-based organisations unique. Faith motivates and energises the work they do. Through faith they discern appropriate ways in which to respond to the communities they serve, whether they be communities of faith, of interest or resident locally... People of faith live out distinct values of trust, respect, and genuine care for those around them.[79]

The Derby Diocese of the Church of England has produced an excellent handbook that provides the theological foundation for mission to the communities around us, ideas for developing a vision for mission and ministry in the community developing your project, the use of buildings, and range of examples.[80]

You may feel you only have resources to do so much and do not wish to overstretch yourself by reaching out in this way. That may seem very commendable after what I have said about the dangers of burnout or poor quality and ill-prepared work. But if our vision for volunteers is limited to filling the coffee rota and finding someone with enough skills and a tough enough skin to be church treasurer, what does that say? This attitude can all too easily lead to a vicious circle (or more accurately, a 'death spiral'). By aiming high, casting a vision, starting small and drawing others in, you may just see your situation transformed.

How carefully have you read the end of Ephesians 1? Tom Wright's translation makes it crystal clear: 'The church is his body; it is the fullness of the one who fills all in all.'[81] In other words, 'King Jesus has, as his hands and feet, his agents within the present world, the church... If only the church would realize this and act accordingly!'[82] That is our calling as Christ's Body: to be at work in God's world, with all the gifts and power he gives us. I pray that this book may play a small part in motivating and mobilising your particular part of the Body to do just that.

Afterword—the story continues

I hope this book will be of use to you as you build up and develop the ministry of the volunteers in your church or organisation. I have tried hard to cover a wide range of relevant issues but no book like this can be completely comprehensive, nor completely up to date.

I know there is so much more wisdom about volunteering out there. You may have been frustrated that I have not covered the particular issue about which you are concerned. You may be saying, 'Yes, but...' to some of the things I have suggested. You may even be disagreeing with me. Let's have a conversation about this, and see what we can learn from each other.

Visit the blog http://churchvolunteer.wordpress.com for an ongoing conversation. Pose your questions, make your points, offer your answers. You are one part of the Body, I am another. 'We have different gifts, according to the grace given to each of us' (Romans 12:6) and we are called to use them as 'each member belongs to all the others' (v. 5). Together we can further help the Body of Christ. I invite you to join me.

Appendix 1:
Web resources

Christian organisations and faith-based sites

Serve
www.serveuk.org

An initiative sponsored by Tear Fund, HOPE, CARE, the Evangelical Alliance and others with the aim of networking and sharing best practice. Offering resources, advice, stories and courses on community involvement and much more. Provides resources covering all aspects of managing community based projects.

Church Urban Fund
www.cuf.org.uk

Long experience in supporting church-run community projects. Provides a comprehensive online resource covering all aspects of project management and much more.

Faith in Action
A resource pack produced by Derby Diocese, 2008

Download it for free from www.faithinderbyshire.org/faith-in-action

Time for God
www.timeforgod.org

Arranges placements for young people in churches.

Faith-based Regeneration Network
www.fbrn.org.uk

Supports local faith-based social action across the UK. The website has a series of worksheets.

Volunteering England
They have some dedicated faith-related pages: www.volunteering.org.uk/component/gpb/faith-related-volunteering

Organisations that support volunteering

National Council for Voluntary Organisations
www.ncvo-vol.org.uk

Provides support and information on all aspects of management for voluntary and community organisations including guidelines on good governance. Offers online training.

KnowHowNonProfit
http://knowhownonprofit.org

Covers all the basics of running a voluntary organisation, including resources, training and advice.

Community Service Volunteers
www.csv.org.uk

Aims to enable people to take an active role in their communities. Offers training and resources, with a focus across the ages and abilities.

The Association of Volunteer Managers
www.volunteermanagers.org.uk

Provides access to a wide range of volunteer management resources and peer networking with other volunteer managers. It is a membership organisation, but volunteers can join for £1.

Our Shared Resources
www.oursharedresources.com

A site containing material relating to working with volunteers, offered by people from all over the world.

Media Trust
www.mediatrust.org

Media Trust is a charity providing communication training for charities, covering a range of media.

Community Matters
www.communitymatters.org.uk

The National Federation for Community Organisations offers training and consultancy; free advice and legal services; business development support; online resources; and a dedicated youth department.

Investing in Volunteers
http://iiv.investinginvolunteers.org.uk

Offers a 'quality standard' for organisations working with volunteers. The process provides a detailed assessment of the provision of care for volunteers. It is suitable for all sizes of organisations and has been used by a variety of faith-based groups.

HRBird for the Third Sector
http://hrbird.org.uk

A useful website that provides links to many other sites with advice on a whole range of personnel issues relating to volunteers and paid staff.

Regional groups in the UK

Volunteering England
www.volunteering.org.uk

Part of NCVO, providing information and resources covering the whole area of volunteering, including a 'Good Practice Bank'.

Wales Council for Voluntary Action
www.wcva.org.uk

Represents and campaigns for voluntary organisations, volunteers and communities in Wales.

Volunteer Now
www.volunteernow.co.uk

Works to promote, enhance and support volunteering across Northern Ireland.

Volunteer Development Scotland
www.vds.org.uk

Works to enhance the practice and improve the quality of the volunteering experience for the people of Scotland.

Websites aimed at encouraging individuals to volunteer

TimeBank
www.timebank.org.uk

Providing volunteers with information on voluntary work and volunteering projects in the UK.

Volunteers Week
www.volunteering.org.uk/policy-and-campaigns/volunteers-week/about-the-week

Make A Difference Day
www.csv.org.uk/campaigns/csv-make-difference-day

'V'
http://vinspired.com

A charity championing youth (16 to 25) volunteering.

National Youth Agency
A site with a wide range of material about working with young people, including links to opportunities for volunteering: www.nya.org.uk/volunteering-what-s-it-all-about

National Citizen Service
www.natcen.ac.uk

Part of the Government's Big Society agenda. Brings 16-year-olds from different backgrounds together in a residential and home-based programme of activity service during the summer.

CSV
www.csv.org.uk

A variety of opportunities for young and older people. Places young people aged 16 and over in voluntary placements away from home (in the UK or abroad) for between four months and a year. CSV's Global Exchange Programme is a six-month programme which gives young people from different countries a unique opportunity to work together and make a practical contribution to local communities.

Background/facts

Institute for Volunteering Research
www.ivr.org.uk

For free reports, visit their Evidence Bank: www.ivr.org.uk/ivr-evidence-bank)

nfpSynergy
www.nfpsynergy.net

Produces free reports and presentations: www.nfpsynergy.net/free-reports-and-presentations

Recruiting/advertising for volunteers

There are many free outlets for volunteer recruitment including your local Volunteer Centre. You can find this via the Volunteering England website (www.volunteering.org.uk), although budget cuts mean there are fewer of these around. Also try your local community websites.

Ivo
http://ivo.org

Carries lists of volunteers offering their services, and also gives groups a chance to share their news.

Reach
www.reachskills.org.uk

Specialises in professionals who offer their services for free.

Do-it
www.do-it.org.uk

This is a general site for people wanting to volunteer and for organisations needing volunteers and also has an employee volunteering section.

Volunteer Genie
www.volunteergenie.org.uk/recruiting-volunteers

Advises on using the media in recruiting. Offers a free book of advice, which can be downloaded here: http://vamu.org.uk/downloads/CleverComms.pdf or you could email them and ask for a hard copy.

International sites

Energize Inc
www.energizeinc.com

American site with lots of free 'bite-sized' chunks of information on a wide variety of topics. Has a linked site: www.e-volunteerism.com (paid subscription to an online journal 'to inform and challenge leaders of volunteers').

Free Management Library

http://managementhelp.org/staffing/volunteers.htm

A lot of American material and from other parts of the world too.

Serviceleader

www.serviceleader.org

A site of the University of Texas, encouraging the study and practice of volunteerism.

International Association for Volunteer Effort

https://iave.org

Promotes volunteering worldwide.

If you want a date on which to peg some focus of volunteering, try these:

International Volunteer Day on 5 December
www.volunteeractioncounts.org/en

International Volunteer Manager's Day on 5 November
www.volunteermanagersday.org

Appendix 2:
Sample policies

Here is a sample volunteer agreement and role description. To adapt them to your own situation ask yourself:

- Is the language too informal/too formal/about right?
- Are all necessary areas included?
- Are all the areas included clear?
- Are all the areas included helpful?
- Are there other areas it would be good to include?
- What length of probationary period would seem right?

Volunteer role description, Anychurch

Volunteering is an important part of being a member of our church. It allows you to use your gifts for the service of God and others. We want you to enjoy your role and hope this role description helps to make clear how we will help you do this, and what is expected of you.

Sunday club assistant

to work with the existing volunteer team, to support the children's work on a Sunday morning (during the 11a.m. service). This takes place in the parish centre.

The work is with children aged 3 to 11 years, encouraging and developing their Christian faith and worship through crafts, games and stories.

Main tasks: sharing in the preparation of resources

planning sessions and assisting in their delivery

Qualities/skills:

good with children

patient

able to work in a team

Training provision:

team training

Diocesan events

others occasionally, if they become available

Commitment: on Sunday—variable, but usually no more than two Sundays every month

meet termly with rest of team to plan activities

Main Point of contact: Children's Work Coordinator (currently Andy Pandy)

Volunteer Agreement, Anychurch

Volunteering is an important part of being a member of our church. It allows you to use your gifts for the service of God and others. We want you to enjoy your role and hope this agreement helps make it clear how we will help you do this, and what is expected of you.

We will:

- always be clear as to what we expect of you (see role description)
- treat you with respect and value your contribution
- listen to your ideas and involve you in discussions about the future development of the work
- provide support, feedback and opportunities for training and development directly required by your role
- respond to any specific requests you may have in order to meet your needs in your role
- provide a safe and healthy environment in which to carry out your duties
- reimburse you for any out of pocket expenses that you are asked to incur
- insure you against any accidental injury you suffer or cause, through our full Public Liability and Volunteer Insurance, while undertaking approved and authorised work
- provide a fair and rapid resolution to any problems, difficulties or grievances that may arise
- be direct and fair if we feel any action by you is detrimental to our work, and allow adequate discussion and time for improvement. We reserve the right to end your involvement if necessary for any reason.
- provide a probationary period of six months, with an opportunity for discussion about how you, and we, feel about your suitability for the role
- provide an annual opportunity for review

We ask you to:

- work in full support of our vision, aims and objectives
- accept the responsibilities set out in the role description
- fulfil your role to the best of your ability
- attend the activity at the agreed times, and to give as much notice as possible if it is ever not possible to do so
- attend training opportunities
- let us know if you would like to change the nature of your involvement
- follow our rules and procedures including those relating to health & safety, safeguarding, equal opportunities and use of personal information
- agree to a Criminal Records Bureau (CRB) check if required
- have due regard for confidentiality
- treat other volunteers, staff, participants and families of participants with courtesy and respect
- recognise that your role is entirely voluntary and is not to be regarded as an employment relationship

Notes

Introduction

1. Phil Hope, Minister of the Third Sector, 15 October 2007
2. The International Association for Volunteer Effort, 16th World Volunteer Conference, January 2001, International Year of Volunteers

Chapter 1: Why people volunteer—and what it offers them in return

3. www.ivr.org.uk/ivr-volunteering-stats
4. When you apply for grants and have to 'match fund', it is more and more common to include the financial equivalent of the volunteer time. You might like to work out the figure for your own church.
5. 'Volunteering trends Jan 08' report from www.nfpsynergy.net. This report also evidences a decline in the numbers of 55- to 64-year-olds volunteering and shows that numbers are static for the over 65s. Interestingly, and encouragingly, there has been an increase among 25- to 34-year-olds. On average, volunteers gave 42 days during 2007—two days up from 2005.
6. http://webarchive.nationalarchives.gov.uk/20120919132719/http://www.communities.gov.uk/publications/communities/2001citizenship survey
7. 'Faith and voluntary action: an overview of current evidence and debates', NCVO, 2007. This report goes into considerable detail about the effects faith has on volunteering, and also about what faith-inspired volunteers have to offer wider society and government policy.
8. Radio 4, *Americana*, 10.10.10. You can read more in his book, David Campbell and Robert D. Putnam, *American Grace—How Religion Divides and Unites Us* (Simon & Schuster, 2010).
9. www.nfpsynergy.net
10. After sports/exercise (34 per cent), children's education/schools (30 per cent) and hobbies/recreation/arts/social clubs (25 per cent), Home Office (2003) 2001 Citizenship Survey
11. www.churchofengland.org/about-us/facts-stats.aspx

12. For example, the classic 'hierarchy of needs' of Abraham Maslow, or the work of David McClelland or Victor Vroom. Also D. Zohar and I. Marshall, *Spiritual Capital: Wealth we can live by* (Bloomsbury, 2005).

13. Robert Putnam, *Bowling Alone: The Collapse and Revival of American Community* (Simon & Schuster, 2001). Although this book focuses entirely on the American volunteering scene, it has a lot more to say that is relevant, because the same trends can be seen here.

14. Jonathan and Thomas McKee, *The New Breed* (Group Publishing, 2008), p. 24.

Chapter 2: Understanding today's volunteers

15. See, for example, the Tomorrow Today website: http://tomorrowtoday. uk.com

16. About 80 per cent of today's grandparents are actively involved in regular childcare, compared with 33 per cent in the 1930s. Thirteen per cent are devoting 20 hours or more to caring for their partner (Elisha Evans and Joe Saxton, 'The 21st Century volunteer', nfpSynergy for the Scout Association, 2005, p. 32).

17. See, for example, Powell and Steinberg, *The Non-Profit Sector, A Research Handbook* (Yale University Press, 2006), who reference several recent studies to prove this point. This point is picked up in the Joseph Rowntree study by Justin Davis Smith and Pat Gray, 'Active ageing in active communities: Volunteering and the transition to retirement': www.jrf.org.uk/publications/volunteering-retirement

18. Smith and Gray, 'Active ageing in active communities: Volunteering and the transition to retirement': www.jrf.org.uk/publications/ volunteering-retirement. Although there are people who take up volunteering at retirement, most are life-long volunteers or come back to volunteering following a break for work and family responsibilities.

19. http://pioneersofchange.net

20. James Lawrence, *Engaging Gen Y* (Grove, 2012), p. 5. This booklet usefully summarises a lot of the issues around Boomers and Generations X and Y.

21. ir2.flife.de/data/natcen-social-research/igb_html/index.php?bericht_ id=1000001&index=&lang=ENG

22. McKee and McKee, *The New Breed*, p. 49.

Chapter 3: Building up the Body of Christ

23. I dislike the current phrase 'work/life balance' since work is part of life, not separate from it. It suggests only the 'life' part is truly valuable. As a volunteer your 'non-work' work is very much part of life. Which side of the 'balance' would that normally fall?
24. Erik Rees, *S.H.A.P.E. Finding & Fulfilling your Unique Purpose for Life* (Zondervan, 2006). This is designed to be used by individuals but it also includes guidelines for using the material as a group.

Chapter 4: Wider ways of volunteering

25. A useful list of tips can be found at: www.fbrn.org.uk/factsheets/play-safe-social-media. For a more detailed discussion see, Richard Moy and Anna Drey, *Leadership and Social Networking: Updating your ministry status* (Grove, 2011).
26. A new version of the Virtual Volunteering Guidebook is to be published soon. See more details at www.coyotecommunications.com/volunteer/guidebook.shtml
27. www.do-it.org.uk. This also has guidelines, ideas and stories from virtual volunteers themselves.
28. See, for example, www.mentalhealthsupport.co.uk/volunteering.html or www.sane.org.uk/how_you_can_help/volunteer
29. The Christian organisation Through the Roof (www.throughtheroof. org) helps people with disabilities to play a full part in church life and helps churches become more aware of issues surrounding people with disabilities. Livability (www.livability.org.uk), formed from John Grooms and the Shaftesbury Society, is a major Christian charity focusing on issues around disabled and disadvantaged people. In 2005 Scope produced a report on disabled people and volunteering: www.scope.org.uk/sites/default/files/pdfs/Volunteering/Scope_disablism_volunteering.pdf
30. An excellent short book emphasising the importance of involving young people in decisions made about youth work is James Vaughton, *Enabling Participation* (Grove, 2012). This is one of a series of booklets covering a variety of topics related to youth work.

31. The Joseph Rowntree study on 'Active ageing' I mentioned earlier (see Note 17) also talks about the significant effect of a strong history of family commitment to volunteering and service.
32. For free home group notes, based on this book, go to www.brfonline. org.uk/extra-resources/
33. Comments from a variety of members of new monastic communities, including Safe Space: www.freshexpressions.org.uk/stories/safespace and Moot: www.moot.uk.net. There are other communities in the UK and many more in the USA: http://newmonasticism.org

Chapter 5: Recruiting your volunteers

34. T. Morgan and T. Stevens, *Simply Strategic Volunteers* (Group Publishing, 2005), p. 123:
35. Romans 12:3–8; 1 Corinthians 12:1–31; 14:1–40; Ephesians 4:7–16; 1 Peter 4:7–11
36. There are many examples freely available on the internet, which you can adapt. Just type in 'church skills survey' into a search engine.
37. Bill Hybels, *The Volunteer Revolution* (Zondervan, 2004), p. 71.
38. Hybels, *Volunteer Revolution*, pp. 67ff.
39. For example, Trinity at Bowes, London—see 'Practical Spirit' (Faith-based Regeneration Network UK, 2010), p. 24. For access to their resources see www.fbrn.org.uk
40. Business in the Community: www.bitc.org.uk. Employee Volunteering: www.employeevolunteering.co.uk might also be able to help direct you to someone in your locality.
41. See Appendix 1 for a list of websites. The national websites may be of limited use, but there are many locally focused ones too.

Chapter 6: Teams, training, trust—and taking risks

42. See, for example, http://en.wikipedia.org/wiki/Tuckman per cent27s_ stages_of_group_development
43. www.myersbriggs.org/my-mbti-personality-type/mbti-basics
44. There are many websites about this. A helpful introduction can be found at http://9types.com/writeup/enneagram.html#intro. Although some Christians have found this a useful method, others have

concerns, because of its assumed basis in Sufism. Personally I find the Myers-Briggs approach much more useful.

45. www.belbin.com

46. www.tmsdi.com

47. You can find out more about these, and other systems, through an internet search.

Chapter 7: A word to leaders

48. Morgan and Stevens, *Simply Strategic Volunteers*, p. 143.

49. Jim Collins, *From Good to Great* (Random House Business, 2001). For others, see the list of 'Best Leadership Books of the 21st Century' complied by MODEM, a Christian leadership network: www.modem-uk.org/bestbooks.html

50. Jim Collins, *Good to Great and the Social Sectors* (Random House, 2006), p. 11.

51. Collins, *Good to Great and the Social Sectors*, p. 9.

52. In a series of books, most recently *Leadership: The Power of Emotional Intelligence: Selected Writings* (More than Sound, 2011). See also *Primal Leadership: Learning to Lead With Emotional Intelligence* (Harvard Business School Press, 2004).

53. D. Goleman, R. Boyatzis and A. McKee, *The New Leaders: Transforming the art of leadership into the science of results* (Little, Brown, 2002), p. x.

54. For an excellent book on humility, I recommend Stephen Cherry's *Barefoot Disciple: Walking the Way of Passionate Humility* (Continuum, 2010). Humility is Jim Collins' deciding factor too—I reckon there is a pattern here.

Chapter 8: The professional problem

55. *Balancing Act: The Challenges and Benefits of Volunteers* (The Urban Institute, December 2004). This is one of a series of reports which, although based on US American research, offer valuable insights and points for reflection.

56. Charles Handy, *Understanding Voluntary Organizations* (Penguin, 1988), p. 6.

57. quoted by Patrick Goh in his blog http://gohbyname.wordpress. com/2013/02/08/yea-ive-been-referred-to-in-a-book-as-and-others/

58. A couple of excellent guides for churches proposing to employ a youth worker are Paul Godfrey and Nic Sheppard, *Employing Youth and Children's Workers: A Guide for Churches* (Church House Publishing, 2008), and Malcolm Herbert and Sally Nash, *Supervising Youth Workers: The Potential and Pitfalls for Churches Employing Youth Workers* (Grove, 2006).

59. Richard Foster, *Celebration of Discipline* (Hodder & Stoughton, 2008), p. 147.

60. For more on Jesus' examples of leadership, see Peter Shaw, *Mirroring Jesus as a Leader* (Grove, 2004).

61. For example, the courses run by 'Livability' (www.livability.org.uk/ church/community-involvement-training-events) or by Volunteering England (www.volunteering.org.uk).

Chapter 9: Practicalities

62. Code of practice for volunteers (Volunteering England, 2012): www. volunteering.org.uk/iwanttovolunteer/code-of-practice-for-volunteers

63. www.cabinetoffice.gov.uk/resource-library/unshackling-good-neighbours

64. The Church Urban Fund has produced a comprehensive booklet called 'Faithfully Volunteering' which you can download for free: http://cuf.org.uk/sites/default/files/Faithfully_Volunteering.pdf. Volunteer England has more—see Note 66.

65. Visit their website: www.ccpas.co.uk. Incidentally, they also deal with other faith groups and indeed with secular organisations.

66. Emlyn Williams, *Reaching and Keeping Volunteers* (Grove, 2006), p. 13.

67. You can find guidance and examples in many places. A good place to start is Volunteer England's website: www.volunteering.org.uk/goo dpractice?q=role+descriptions. Some items are freely downloadable, others for members only. Your local volunteer centre should be able to advise you about developing a volunteering policy. See appendix for a sample.

68. See appendix for a sample.

Chapter 10: Saying 'thank you'

69. I have my doubts over the wisdom of such things for adults. If you are interested, there are companies that will supply pretty much any gift you could think of (and many you would not) overprinted with your church or charity's name. If you are going to give a gift, then I suggest making it a useful one.

Chapter 11: Problems, conflict and ending well

70. For courses on listening see www.acornchristian.org/listening
71. C.S. Lewis, *The Problem of Pain*, 1940.
72. That is a very small example of the issue of change. Introducing change can cause a lot of conflict and dis-ease, and if you want to read up on Change Management, I recommend George Binney and Colin Williams, *Leaning into the Future: Changing the way people change organisations* (Nicolas Brealey, 1997). Although is aimed squarely at the business world, it poses the question, 'Is it reasonable to hope that people should derive [most] fulfilment from their lives at work?' (p.167). Substitute 'volunteering' for 'work' and for many volunteers the answer may well be 'yes'. It also looks at such things as 'working with the grain', encouraging learning within an organisation, which involves a lot of listening, and of 'giving away power to become more powerful', especially key, I would suggest, in regards to volunteers.
73. White hat (information known or needed), Red hat (emotions, hunches and intuition), Black hat (critical judgment, devil's advocate), Yellow hat (benefits, optimism), Green hat (creativity, possibilities, alternatives), Blue hat (managing the thinking process, deciding when the other five should be used). See for example www.debonogroup. com/six_thinking_hats.php

Chapter 12: Beyond the church walls

74. Ann Morisy, *Journeying Out* (Continuum, 2004), p. 195.
75. Morisy, *Journeying Out*, p. 86.
76. www.sa-cni.org.uk
77. www.streetpastors.co.uk

78. See for example, 'Face to Face and Side by Side: a framework for partnership in our multi faith society', Department for Communities and Local Government, 2008. This approach has been continued by the current government.

79. Jane Winter, *Interactive Project Development for Faith-Based Organisations Involved in Social Action* (Faith-based Regeneration Network UK, 2010).

80. *Faith in Action* (Derby Diocese, 2008) A CD can be purchased or the material downloaded for free from http://faithinderbyshire.org/faith-in-action

81. Tom Wright, *Paul for Everyone: The Prison Letters* (SPCK, 2004), p. 14.

82. Wright, *Paul for Everyone*, p. 17.

Enjoyed
this book?

Write a review—we'd love to hear what you think.
Email: reviews@brf.org.uk

Keep up to date—receive details of our new books as they happen.
Sign up for email news and select your interest groups at:
www.brfonline.org.uk/findoutmore/

Follow us on Twitter @brfonline

By post—to receive new title information by post (UK only), complete
the form below and post to: BRF Mailing Lists, 15 The Chambers, Vineyard,
Abingdon, Oxfordshire, OX14 3FE

Your Details
Name _____
Address_____
_____
Town/City _____ Post Code _____
Email_____

Your Interest Groups (*Please tick as appropriate)

❏ Advent/Lent	❏ Messy Church
❏ Bible Reading & Study	❏ Pastoral
❏ Children's Books	❏ Prayer & Spirituality
❏ Discipleship	❏ Resources for Children's Church
❏ Leadership	❏ Resources for Schools

Support your local bookshop
Ask about their new title information schemes.